The Momentum Framework

Grow your business & dominate the market in any economy

Wayne Fox

Copyright © 2024 Wayne Fox. All rights reserved.

No part of this book may be reproduced in any form without permission in writing from the Author. Reviewers may quote brief passages in reviews.

Disclaimer and FTC Disclaimer

No part of this publication may be reproduced or transmitted in any form or by any means, mechanical or electronic, including photocopying or recording, by any information storage and retrieval system, or by email without permission in writing from the publisher.

While all attempts have been made to verify the information provided in this publication, the Author does not assume any responsibility for errors, omissions, or contrary interpretations of the subject matter herein.

This book is for entertainment purposes only. The views expressed are those of the Author and should not be taken as expert instruction or commands. The reader is responsible for their actions.

Adherence to all applicable laws and regulations, including international federal, state, and local governing professional licensing, business practices, advertising, and all other aspects of doing business in the US, Canada, UK, or any other jurisdiction, is the sole responsibility of the purchaser or reader.

The Author does not assume any responsibility or liability whatsoever on behalf of the purchaser or reader of this material.

Any perceived slight of any individual or organization is purely unintentional. I sometimes use affiliate links with the content of the book. This means I will be paid a sales commission if you make a purchase. This, however, does not mean my opinion is for sale. Any affiliate links listed in the book are the services and products for which I've used myself and found beneficial. The reader or purchaser should do their research before making a purchase online.

Contents

1.0 What others are saying

2.0 Introduction

3.0 Part One - Building the foundation

3.1 Introduction to the IMPACT Foundation™

3.2 Building the foundation

3.3 Intelligence

3.4 Model

3.5 Product

3.6 Asset

3.7 Cash

3.8 Team

3.9 The improvement plan

3.10 Summary

4.0 Part Two - The growth stage

4.1 Intro to the growth stage

4.2 Growing shareholder value

4.3 The five stages of a small business

4.4 Level one: Compass

4.5 Level two: Community

4.6 Level three: Club

4.7 Level four: Credentials

4.8 Level five: Credibility

4.9 Level six: Confidence

4.10 Level seven: Client

4.11 Level eight: Compensation

4.12 Level nine: Capital

4.13 Level ten: Compound

4.14 The bottleneck

4.15 The secret ingredients

4.16 Summary

5.0 Conclusion

6.0 About the author

What others are saying

Your reviews go here

Introduction

Monday 11th October 1999, a few months after my 20th birthday, & I'd just returned to the Scottish Highlands after working in Nottingham for five months. For the previous four years, five months, and eight days, I'd pestered my Dad to let me be more involved in running our family business, a small Electrical contractor. More specifically, I wanted to be involved in growing the business because this is what inspired me. By this point in my career, I'd qualified as an Electrician; my Dad had insisted I needed to focus on learning the technical side of the business before I could think about anything else. My return to Scotland was the *'Zero point'* in our growth journey, of winning contracts all over Scotland, & becoming a recognized player in the industry.

I'd been working in Nottingham to gain experience of delivering larger projects, from large-scale new housing developments to refurbishing Nottingham University.

But whilst I had all the enthusiasm in the world, & bags of ideas, we didn't know what ideas or strategies to choose, as the business, whilst it had been trading in Scotland for the previous ten years, had employed a few people previously, but essentially at this point, it was just the two of us, with my Mum working in the office a few days a week too. This eventually meant we would go through lots of trial & error, seeing what worked, &

what didn't, with most activities making no impact on the business, whilst a handful of activities would catapult the business forward.

As we got better at identifying what worked, we used the process in other businesses and tested other advanced strategies. I've since used this same process across multiple industries, both B2B (Business to Business) and B2C (Business to Consumer) customer types, Renewable energy to Media to Hospitality. Whilst we grew each of these businesses to become significant players in their respective industry, achieving multi-million-pound revenue, within a few years, every time we did it, the results would happen faster and faster, as we cut out all of that *'trial & error'*, but as a by-product of that, we also reduced all the unnecessary costs of the growth process too.

In the last decade, I've come into contact with well over 1,000 small business owners. About 98% of them all share the same genes when it comes to a conversation around growth. They fall into three categories; the first is those that seem caught in the headlights. There are just too many options to choose from. Should they do Facebook ads, write a book, or do SEO on their website? Maybe they should follow that guy online, telling them to buy a business instead? Ultimately, in the end, this group is too overwhelmed to do anything. Hence, they tick along, usually surviving on their past reputation & word of mouth in the local community, and that's as far as their growth journey goes. The problem with this route is that it's difficult to plan for the business, and it's difficult to commit to employing more staff.

These companies can't accurately predict whether they'll have enough work to employ staff in the future, so they end up with *'yo-yo staff'*, employing someone when it gets busy, but a few months later having to let them go because the workload has fallen off a cliff. This was our business before that *'zero point'* in 1999. This problem is what makes it so difficult to attract and retain staff because those employees know the job might not last.

The second category are those who get stuck doing something that doesn't work. They see lots of noise and apparent *'success'* from other people who get great results, and so they jump into it, only to spend lots of time and money and never get anywhere with it. This is like chasing the shiny penny, and it ultimately leads to people believing they aren't good at *'this business malarkey.'*

Finally, the third category is those who go through trial and error, trying everything and eventually figuring out what works and what's just fluff and noise from the industry gurus. This was our path, and while we got there in the end, it took lots of time, money, and commitment to see it through, which most people aren't willing to make. Would you spend the next ten years spending hundreds of thousands of pounds and countless hours, with NO guarantee of ever reaching the promised land?

My intention in writing this book is to provide you with a blueprint to understand where you are now and what the best strategy is for your business, without going through that trial-and-error process.

Unlike the hundreds of coaching books & programs available, I have no interest in coaching anyone through the process; I've got nothing to sell you. This book isn't part of an *'upsell chain'* of products; I'm not interested in any of that; honestly, the thought of doing that sends me into a boredom-induced deep sleep. However, if reading the book attracts a potential joint venture partner to work on our projects or a business owner who wants to sell *'his baby'* to a safe pair of hands, that would be great. The book is written to provide everything you need without signing up for a gold-level mentoring program.

Until around 2019, this framework did not exist anywhere in physical form. It was just something I instinctively did with every business I've been involved with. But in 2019, I had an idea to create a business accelerator program, providing investment & growth support to small businesses, using this process to grow each of those businesses. To do that, I needed to formalize the process, get it out of my head, & put it down on paper so anyone could use it. This process was easier said than done. So after analyzing every business, every project, every scenario, & understanding what we'd done each time, I eventually went through over 300 different scenarios, & mapped them all out into what we now call the Momentum Framework™.

It's called the Momentum Framework™ because the process is designed to build momentum. It's designed like a pyramid, with the most significant impact being made at the highest levels of the pyramid. So choosing a strategy at stage ten in the framework will ultimately see the most significant & fastest results for your business, but to use a strategy at that level, you need to have the other lower levels covered first, hence the idea of building momentum in the business. This is where our trial-and-error experience adds value to the process.

The framework starts in Part One with the IMPACT Foundation™. This stage is about building a strong foundation for the business. Without this foundation, if you try to grow the business, the business can collapse at anytime. You wouldn't build a pyramid without first having a solid foundation.

After establishing the foundation, we can focus on the ten steps to climbing the pyramid. We call this the Ten C's Framework™. Towards the end of the book, I've included a couple of bonus chapters; I call these *'the bottleneck'* and *'the secret ingredients'*. I know you'll really enjoy these, and I've deliberately left them until the end so they have maximum effect on your business.

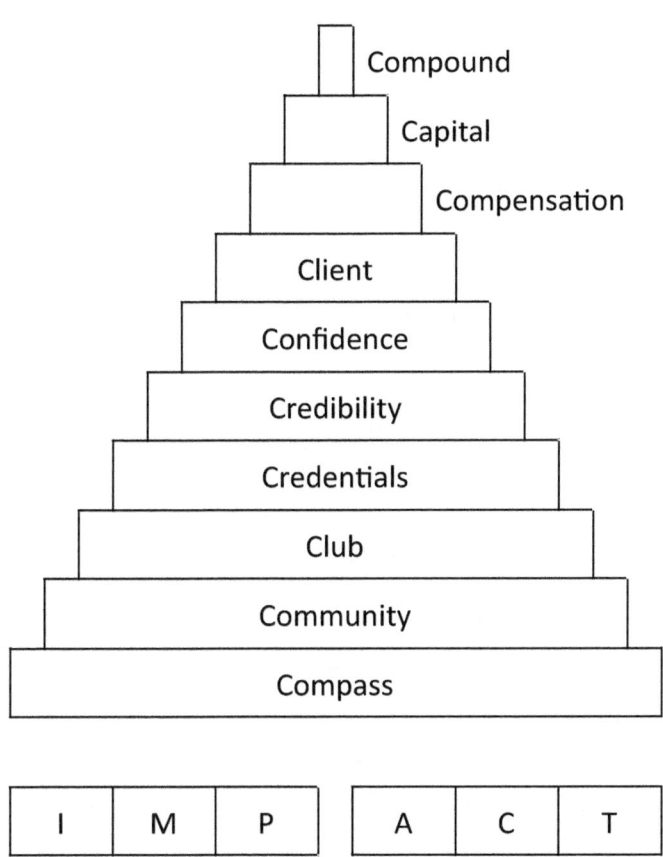

Part One

Building a foundation

Introduction to the IMPACT Foundation™

The financial aspects of a business are fundamental to building a solid foundation in any company. Within the foundation-building process, we use a framework called the IMPACT Foundation™ to construct the six business foundations.

The IMPACT Foundation™ is a model for building a solid foundation for any business, enabling it to grow sustainably. Often, when a small business experiences some growth, it will fall back to where it was previously or, in some cases, go out of business completely. This is because it hasn't built a solid foundation; it's the equivalent of trying to build a house on quicksand. Our IMPACT Foundation™ takes you through the six areas of building that foundation for the business.

I: Intelligence - Understanding what's going on in the business

M: Model - Looking at the Business model. Is it still relevant & can it be improved

P: Product - What does your customer experience

A: Asset - Protecting what you've already got

C: Cash - The objective is to improve the financial position of the business

T: Team - A group of people coming together to achieve a common goal

Building the foundation

Our foundation program shares many of the same processes as a business turnaround. We discovered that the same outcomes were achieved, whether the business was in financial distress or financially strong. Everyone wants more money in the bank and a strong balance sheet, right?

Much like a house, part of the reason a business gets into financial distress is that it doesn't have a foundation in place or because the foundation hasn't been maintained over time. So, when we perform a business turnaround, we're essentially building the same blocks that enable the business to flourish later on. I think of it as less of a business turnaround and more of a foundation for growth.

The only difference between a financially healthy business going through this process is that the healthy business hasn't experienced that trigger event, forcing it to become a turnaround case. Building the foundation in either case means you don't need to worry about that trigger event happening, as you'll have a strong business to weather whatever storms may arrive in the future.

Be careful where you take advice

I see people posting on their Facebook or LinkedIn pages asking people what they should do. A recent example was a business owner asking for advice about selling their engineering business. They'd been approached by someone looking to buy an engineering business, and he was asking his Facebook friends what to do. There followed hundreds of comments from people, '*advising*' him not to accept the deal because of '*X*' or instead counteroffer with '*Y*'.

These people were not experts in buying a business. They had no experience of the subject, and some had never even run a business. They were average Joe's.

Everyone's an expert on social media platforms. It's usually those with either the loudest voice or the biggest marketing budget who get heard. Much of the time, their advice comes with bias, sometimes even jealousy. We wouldn't walk up to a random stranger in the street and ask their advice, so why do people do it on social media?

Business isn't difficult

Some people believe business is tricky. Business is fun—a challenge, but fun. I've learnt that there's always someone who has already done what you want to do. It might not be the exact same story, but similarities can be taken and generally tweaked to achieve what you want to achieve, very quickly.

If you have a framework for reaching the end goal, whether that's turning a business around, growing a business, raising investment, or selling a business, if you have that step-by-step formula to follow, you, too, can achieve any of those things, and much more besides.

The process

The severity of the need to build your business foundation has four key stages, which I demonstrate using the medical analogy.

1. Recognize the need for it.
2. A&E - Fix any emergency, stop the bleeding, buy time
3. Intensive care - Get it off life support, Get money in the bank
4. Physio - Build a strong foundation for the future

If the business is already healthy, you focus only on the last two stages. But this is why it shares much of the same process as performing a complete business turnaround.

The options

When a business recognizes it has a need, depending on how bad it is, it has four options to deal with the problem. This is the same whether the business is in distress or financially healthy. Without a strong foundation, a trigger event will send it into a distressed state. Here are the options:

1. Fix the business, going through the process we'll talk about
2. Sell the business, getting whatever you can for it, but essentially passing the problem to someone else
3. Shut it down, assuming it can meet its current obligations
4. Appoint an insolvency practitioner if it can't meet its obligations

Everything we discuss here is intended to be done before the business reaches the insolvency practitioner stage. Sometimes, even if a company can't pay the monthly payroll, some things can be done before it reaches that stage, assuming you take action quickly instead of burying your head in the sand.

Often, when an insolvency practitioner contacts me, the business is already past saving. In such a case, they're just going through a process of liquidating assets, to pay any creditors.

What are your long-term plans?

When I meet a business owner for the first time, I always like to ask them what their long-term plans are for their lives. I'm generally talking about the next 5-10 years because this should influence their decisions about which option to pursue.

Sometimes, a business owner will tell me they plan to sell the business, but they must fix their financial hole first. In such instances, I always suggest that perhaps it's better to work with someone with the experience of turning a business around and let them take that responsibility on; in the meantime, they'll get to know the company, & when you're ready to sell in three or four years, you'll have a motivated buyer that'll be happy to buy your shares. This route also saves much of the costs relating to selling the business.

The majority of businesses are fundamentally the same. The overall rule of business is that all businesses share the same fundamentals:
- All businesses sell something
- There's a cost to deliver that product
- There's a cost to running the business
- The difference between the selling price and the total costs is the profit.

If these fundamentals are the same, you'd expect two businesses in the same industry to be relatively identical; still, as we know, that's never the case. Why does most of the high street struggle to stay afloat, while Amazon has bumper profits, yet they're both in the same industry?

The reason is what's inside that middle section, between the selling price and the profit: how it delivers those products, how it delivers the back office support, and how it charges for that product.

The slide from health into distress

When I was a child, my grandad always said, *'If the business isn't growing, it's dying.'* I didn't understand then how it could be dying if its sales stayed the same. Thirty-five years later, I understand what he meant. The problem with stagnant sales is that it doesn't consider the economy or your competitors.

If the economy grows by 5% a year, your business must also increase by 5% to stay the same in real terms. Otherwise, it's shrinking in real terms. The next point is about your competition.

If each of your competitors grows by 10% each year, but you stay the same size, they're all increasing their market share compared to your business. Project this pattern over many years, and over time, your market share will reduce every year, eventually falling to zero. As your competitors grow, they also attract staff from those firms that aren't growing.

Another side effect of not growing your business, which I've seen firsthand, is when your client's business grows. Hence, they naturally need you to grow to meet their increased demand. This is growing by association with them. By refusing to grow with them, they eventually choose to go to your competitors. This touches on what we're about to look at—stagnation!

Signs of future distress

Whilst it isn't always easy to spot a business's impending doom when you're shoulder-deep on the front line, there are some tell-tale stages that, if not recognized, usually lead to eventual failure.

1. Stagnation or Decline in Sales / Profit
2. Distress
3. Crisis
4. Failure

Sometimes, everything seems good until a trigger event occurs and shakes the business to its core. I saw this with a few of our competitors in the 2009 global financial crisis. Whilst they appeared from the outside to be doing okay before the recession hit, as soon as clients started to delay payment or sales inevitably reduced, as they do in recessions, the cracks began to appear in their business. During a change in the economy, most companies tend to be slow to react & maintain the same overheads, which drains cash from the business.

Less cash flowing in the business eventually leads to the inability to pay suppliers and staff on time. This subsequently leads to a tighter cash restriction, and the business owner's attention and focus are taken away as they scramble to fix it. What's happening is that they're robbing Peter to pay Paul while dodging bullets from the friendly bailiffs. It's a downward spiral that you can't fix from within it.

Symptoms of an impending problem

One of the easiest ways to catch a problem before it erodes the business is to spot the symptoms. You can spot the same symptoms in your business by looking at the most common symptoms a company goes through as it goes into the Slide. The trick is to be objective, however. Over 80% of small businesses experience these symptoms, so sometimes it's better to let your staff identify them, as they don't have the same emotional connection to the company as its owner, so they can be more objective.

Symptoms of impending distress
- Loss in market share
- Loss of reputation (more client complaints)
- Stagnant / reducing sales revenue (Annual / Monthly / TTM)
- Stagnant / reducing profit margin (Annual / Monthly / TTM)
- Increasing overhead as a percentage of revenue
- Making losses on contracts
- Banks demanding more information about the business
- Suppliers reduce credit terms
- Supplier accounts frozen or on-stop
- Credit cards rejected at check-out
- The bank requests more security
- Staff turnover rising / Unhappy staff
- Increasing need to borrow money
- Need to invest more capital to fund trading
- Overdraft increasing
- Stretch creditor payment terms
- Factored debt never reduces
- Bidding lower margins to win contracts
- Accounts filed later & later

- The bank requests more regular meetings
- The bank requests financial projections
- The bank requests more personal guarantees
- The bank requests someone to look into the situation
- Bidding for *'Monumental'* contracts, hoping one contract will turn things around

Symptoms of the crisis state
- Finance director off sick / leaves employment
- Overdraft at its limit
- Cheques bouncing
- The bank requests some repayment
- Delaying payments to creditors
- Borrowing on personal loans/credit cards to fund the business
- Statutory payments (VAT, PAYE, Tax) in arrears
- Legal action, writs, CCJ's Winding up orders
- Bailiffs
- Debt collection letters

- Insolvency practitioner letters asking if they can help
- Landlord unhappy with unpaid rent

I've created a set of 12 questions to determine how healthy a business is.

1. Is the industry going through change or disruption?
2. Are our clients' industries going through change or disruption?
3. Do you worry about paying staff/suppliers every month?
4. Are you hoping for the next client to turn things around?
5. Have suppliers frozen your account or reduced your credit terms?
6. Have suppliers issued legal proceedings/debt collection/bailiff against you?
7. Do you lack vital management personnel in any of the five core areas?

8. Do your clients make up more than 5% of your total revenue?
9. Are your financial reporting systems weak or need improving?
10. Has the business suffered a significant event (client bankruptcy, fraud, fire, theft, death)?
11. Are you working more than 50 hours per week but still not getting things completed?
12. Are you constantly faced with problems & firefighting in the business?

Hopefully, you'll see some areas for improvement, and this is where the foundation-building process starts: fixing any identified problems and reinforcing what you already have.

Intelligence

The Intelligence stage is the first and, in my opinion, one of the most important sections of the IMPACT Foundation™. The primary objective of the Intelligence stage is to gather as much data about the business as possible, hopefully creating a system where the data is updated daily rather than being static and frozen in time.

Let's look at some areas we must consider for the Intelligence stage.

The root cause

If you've got a problem or recurring issue in the business, the first thing you need to do is discover the root cause of that problem before you can fix it. It's easy to assume that the cause of a problem is the immediate culprit, but most often, that's just a symptom of a much deeper cause. The easiest way to find the root cause is to look at the problem and ask *'WHY'* this happened, *'WHY'* is this the case? Let's look at an example.

Example.
Problem: The client is unhappy and claiming from you for losses incurred to their business
WHY?
Cause 1: Contract not delivered on time
WHY?

Cause 2: Staff unable to buy equipment from suppliers

WHY?

Cause 3: Company account on-stop

WHY?

Cause 4: Sheila in Accounts didn't pay the supplier invoice

WHY?

Cause 5: There weren't sufficient funds in the bank

WHY?

Cause 6: Clients haven't paid their invoices

WHY?

Cause 7: Invoices weren't sent out on time

WHY?

Cause 8: We didn't have all the info needed to create the invoice

WHY?

Cause 9: We have poor systems to manage client accounts

WHY?

Cause 10: We've been more focused on winning clients than building systems

WHY?

Cause 11: The business owner is biased towards sales, as that's his skill set

In this example, it took eleven *'why's* before discovering the root cause of the problem. Normally, you can get to the root cause within 5 *'whys'*. If you've ever hit a problem and tried to fix the immediate cause, you'll know the problem doesn't go away; most of the time, it'll appear elsewhere. It's because you need to go deeper to discover the REAL cause.

A word of warning: Sometimes, you might not like the answer, especially if the fault lies with you. This is your chance to be honest with yourself. Do you really want to fix the problem once and for all, or do you prefer to keep dancing around the elephant in the room and protect your ego?

Client analysis

When was the last time you took a rational look at each client? How about each of your contracts? What I've found is that most businesses don't analyze their clients. The problem with this, to be blunt, is that some clients aren't worth it. They carry very low-profit margins, contributing very low amounts of profit to the bottom line. By measuring how profitable each client & contract is and what the profit contribution is to the bottom line, you can make decisions about the future strategy for the business based on fact rather than emotion. As an advanced metric, measuring the overhead associated with each client is important, as some clients require a lot of effort and resources to manage their accounts, whereas others require very little.

Product analysis

Next, we need to analyze your business's product offerings. How much profit do we make from each product offering?

When discussing product offerings, I'm talking about the products, services, or experiences your clients buy from you. Every business should have multiple product offerings, whether an overnight stay in a hotel bedroom, a new central heating system, or a design for building a new house, depending on its type.

You may have a range of product offerings, some with very high margins and some with very low margins. When you have this information, one step you might take could be to cut the low-margin products instead just focusing on investing in the high-margin offerings. There's no blanket answer, though, as some offerings may complement others, so removing one product offering could also force demand for the higher-margin offerings to reduce in number.

Removing low-margin offerings may result in removing clients from the business, too. Occasionally, you use the low-margin product offerings to entice new clients, leading them to buy the higher-margin offerings. Every business is different in this regard, depending on the business model. However, if 90% of your business capacity is spent delivering low-margin products, & one of your main problems is finding new staff, removing a low-margin product should free up some of your existing staff time, solving some of your staff demand issues. If you can use technology or outsource the low-margin products, this could be a way to deliver them without having to dedicate your resources. By having the information at your fingertips, you can make those choices.

Every product offering has a buyer trend. Some product offerings will be more popular during certain months or seasons, such as Winter. If you're a hotel operator, the room demand might be very low in Q1 but high in Q2 & Q3. What is the buyer trend for your product offerings? To make this easier to spot, you can analyze it on a quarterly, six-monthly & annual basis for each product offering. The more granular you can make this analysis, the easier it is to make decisions.

In addition to seasonal cycles, you may discover that demand for a particular offering increases or declines over time. Knowing this information, you can predict how each offering will impact the company's revenue over the coming months and years. Whilst you might not predict the whole market, measuring demand by the number of enquiries you receive for each product will give you an idea of where things are going.

Another tool you can use for this, more so for online product offerings, is Google Trends. This tool shows how many people are searching for a particular term, for example, *'accounting services'*. If the search term trended up over a long period, the offering would be increasing in demand. It will be difficult to get into the specifics of every product offering you have unless your entire business is online. Still, it might show a trend for the whole industry.

Reporting

Part of knowing where you are in a business comes down to reporting. Without this information kept up to date, it's impossible to make decisions in the business. As a starting point, a company should produce reports regularly, providing shareholders & senior staff members with up-to-date information about the business. Ideally, these reports would be available on a *'live'* basis. However, producing them every month would give you a good level of insight.

As with everything, the reports are only as good as the information entered into them.

Here's the type of information that should be produced in the reports:

- Financial pack
    - Profit & Loss (consolidated & broken down by client, contract & product)
    - Balance sheet
    - Aged debtors & creditors
    - Projected Profit & Loss
    - Projected cash flow forecast
    - Financial ratios
- Management pack
    - Sales report
        - Actions, Prospects, Sales visits planned, Average contract value, product-by-product sales, client breakdown, order pipeline, conversion rate

- Operations
    - Utilization & efficiency rate, stockouts, customer satisfaction

With each of these reports, it can be easy to go too granular, looking at lots of numbers that mean very little. One method to fix this is creating a traffic light-based dashboard with indicators for each Red, Orange, & Green metric. If the indicator is Green, the status is good & we don't need to worry about it. If it's Red, we know there's a real danger and must fix the problem immediately. If an indicator is Orange, we know something's happened that we need to investigate & bring back to total health again.

The average business wouldn't know they'd hit a problem until the alarm bells are ringing. Still, with a dashboard system like this, you can identify changes early and fix them before they escalate into a significant problem for the business.

Bank foreclosure ratios

Another benefit of a reporting system is identifying problems before others know about them. Banks and other lending institutions use several indicators and ratios to analyze when a business might get into trouble.

To the average business owner, a financial ratio means nothing. Yet, a slight change in such a metric can mean a bank or other lenders can call in its lending facility, or suppliers can reduce your credit terms.

The 80/20 principle

There is a common rule in the universe called the 80/20 Pareto Principle. This theory says that 80% of your output will come from 20% of your input. In other words, 80% of your revenue will come from 20% of your clients. 80% of your profits will come from 20% of your contracts. This is true across all areas of life and business; try it out in your own business and see what I mean.

It's this same principle that elite athletes use when training for events. They understand that all they need to do is identify the 20% portion of what they do and focus on improving that portion. For an Olympic swimmer, that might be the turn. If a swimmer can shave 5 seconds off their time by perfecting their turn, that'll put them two or three lengths ahead of their competitors. To perfect their turn might mean focusing solely on building their leg muscles. Again, how they perfect their turn will come down to the 80/20 principle of what they focus on. This ultimately comes down to the advanced 96/4 principle, where 96% of the result comes from just 4% of the activity. It's the advanced Pareto principle - The 20% of the 20%.

This is where it gets exciting. Imagine winning the Olympic gold medal by figuring out what that 4% of activity is and focusing on that. While your competitors are training 18 hours a day, trying to improve every area of their skill, you're focused on just that 4%, and by doing that, you can beat them. Understanding this principle means you can improve your results with less effort than focusing on everything. The key is determining what activities makeup 20% of the activity.

One example is when I created an online course a few years ago. To test the principle, I promoted the course across 800 different marketing channels, including various Facebook groups and LinkedIn groups, as well as working with influencers. With each marketing channel, I created a tracking code for it so that when people purchased the course, I knew where that lead came from. After three months, I analyzed the results, and as if by magic, I found approximately 150 of those marketing channels gave me some form of result; the other 650 gave me less than two leads each. I then did the advanced 96/4 analysis, & again, the same magic happened. Around 30 of those marketing channels were bringing me nearly all my leads. The time & money invested into all of these different marketing channels would have been unsustainable over a long period, but knowing I only had to focus on thirty of them to achieve almost the same results meant that I could forget about the rest. That freed up weeks & weeks' worth of work in promoting each marketing channel.

ROTLC (Return on Total Life Costs)

With every type of business, there'll be a metric to measure performance. With a supermarket, it might be *'revenue per cubic feet'*. With a service business, it might be *'gross profit per employee'*. For a hair salon, the metric might be *'revenue per seat'* or, even better, *'profit per seat, per hour'*. It doesn't matter what you choose to measure so long as it is the main driver for your business.

To give you an example of how you might calculate this in your own business, let's consider the example of a large country estate, considering revenue, capital value, costs, profit and returns for various choices of land usage on that estate.

	Revenue	Cost	Profit	ROTLC
Farm Land	120,000	30,000	90,000	x3
Business Units	2m	50,000	1.95m	x39
Rented Housing	300,000	20,000	280,000	x14
Solar Farm	1.5m	600,000	900,000	x1.5

All of these numbers are made up for this example. Still, if these were real numbers in our business, we could see that the best return comes from the business units and the rented housing. With this example, we've ignored any change in capital value. Still, in such a case, you should look at the total lifetime revenue, capital value, and costs for a fairer comparison.

By breaking your business down into areas or product offerings like this, you can identify which generates the highest return and then invest more of your time and money into those areas.

Industry trends

To plan our future, we must understand the larger macro trends that will impact our business in the long term. To oppose these more significant macro trends would be like trying to force water uphill.

My intention is to make you aware of the drivers and guide you in spotting potential hazards your business might face on its growth journey.

Around 2013, I became interested in watching trends and how everything seemed to follow a predictable pattern over many years, sometimes over entire generations. Then, I discovered the law of cause & effect. These are the two guidestones to predicting the future.

My first introduction to seeing repeating patterns was in the property market. Seeing the hype around the property market and everyone clambering to get in, just as it was reaching its peak in 2007, only to crash by 40%, leaving all those people badly burnt and in negative equity. But looking back over time, the same thing happened repeatedly every 15 years or so. Still, every time it happened, people were shocked by it, as if it was a new phenomenon. More importantly, why do people have such short memories & why don't they learn from their mistakes the first time?

After that point, I went down the rabbit hole when I discovered someone named Roger Hamilton, who was based in Bali. He called himself a Futurist. I remember wondering what a futurist was and how amazing it would be if you knew what would happen, especially in business. Imagine the possibilities of knowing the future.

The funny thing was that everything that Roger predicted happened within 12-18 months, and he didn't just do it once; he predicted correctly year after year. I started to believe he must be a time traveller. But when you realize the process, whilst it takes time, anyone can see, at least, a vague glimpse into the future.

Case study: Home furnishings supplier

Working with a local home furnishings specialist, they offered a range of products, including various flooring types, such as traditional carpet, wood flooring, and ceramic stone floors. In addition to flooring, they also sold hard furnishings, including beds, sofas, and curtains.

As part of their carpet range, they had around 40 different designs and supporting products, including underlay, carpet gripper rods, & door jointing strips. The carpet range consisted of three price categories: the budget range, the mid-range, and the premium range - the premium range was the type of carpet you might find in a castle or stately home, with a pile thicker than an Inuit's coat. Whilst the latter was a lot more expensive for customers to buy, it also carried quite a high overhead expense, as it didn't sell very often compared to the other two price ranges.

The first step was to narrow down the carpet design choices. Most had around the same profit margins, so the selection came down to popularity. Out of the 40 designs, only 8 of them sold regularly. Removing the remaining 32 designs enabled the sales staff to focus on promoting the big sellers.

The next stage was removing the premium carpets from the offering, which meant the business didn't have to hold much stock. An on-demand order system was created to meet the occasional castle owner's needs. The product was manufactured as the customer ordered it and delivered directly to the property, meaning the business would never come into contact with it until it was installed.

After analyzing the other product lines, we identified that the ceramics range carried the highest margins. The buyer trend towards stone flooring products has increased in the previous three years. In contrast, the buyer trend for carpets & laminate flooring had been reducing.

By utilizing the extra space created by reducing the carpet product offerings, the company could introduce a larger ceramics & stone range to the product offering.

Model

The Model section of the IMPACT Foundation™ is focused on the business model. Is the business model relevant in today's changing economy, or can it be adapted & improved?

Suppose you look at the past decade's well-publicized examples of business failures. In that case, one you might notice, above all others, is the rapid decline of the high street.

The high street retail business model started declining when the internet shopping era emerged. This happened because people wanted convenience. They no longer wanted to spend half their day driving to the high street, finding a parking space, paying for that parking, then walking around shops, trying to find what they needed, only to be told *'the item's out of stock, but it might be back in next week'*.

Instead of suffering tired feet, & lots of frustration, they could get everything they wanted online in ten minutes and then wait for it to be delivered. Whilst the online model was clunky to begin with, for those who noticed it, this should have been a stark warning sign that this was where the retail industry was heading. Only some adapted to create online versions of their physical stores, but most did not.

Walk down most high streets now, & you'll see the battered remains of a tired and struggling industry. On my local high street, there's a well-known stationary shop, a card shop, a jewellery store, and about ten cafes and food takeaways. The rest are empty former banks, travel agents, & clothes shops. But look deeper into the financials of those that remain, all of them being part of nationwide retail chains, & you'll notice many of them haven't made a profit in over ten years.

They seem to be using a tactic to finance those ongoing trading losses by selling off parts of the business, borrowing cheap debt, or selling shares in the company. These companies will inevitably not be around by the turn of the decade, either.

The same principle applies to supermarkets. We'll see this industry move entirely online in the coming years. It makes sense. Retail space is expensive—rent, rates, running costs, staff costs, and minimal choice for the consumer. Online space is very cheap in comparison. The current online version of supermarkets is based around selling whatever is available in that local store, having staff go around the store picking it, and then delivering it to the customer's house - this is not an e-commerce business model, & brings lots of inefficiencies.

Compare this to the online shopping companies that have never had a physical retail store. *Amazon* has giant warehouses all over the country. They have unlimited choices on their website. In some cases, orders are picked by robotic systems. Warehousing costs a fraction of the equivalent sized retail space. This will inevitably be the moment when the supermarket experience of the future will move. These traditional supermarkets can adapt; they too have giant warehouses already, but instead of shipping, in bulk, out to each supermarket, they'll need to follow Amazon's example of picking single unit items in the warehouse, perhaps also using robotics instead of manual labour. This will be a massive hurdle for them to overcome, as many of their warehouses are sized perfectly for what they already do, so transitioning to this new model may mean expanding their current facilities, & slowly phasing out delivery to local stores. If they don't adapt, they'll die over the next decade.

But this all boils down to their chosen business model. Many small businesses never consider their business model. Many run their business almost unconsciously, doing the same as every other business in their industry. They often follow the same business model used in their industry for over 100 years.

Designing a business model isn't easy, and I can't provide an instruction manual in this short space.

Still, there is one area you can start. First, you must recognize that your industry will be radically disrupted over the next decade. Keep an eye on new market entrants, especially those with strong financial backing. You can copy these companies or redesign your business model to compete against these new entrants.

I created a concept called the *'Four types of company'*. I've created videos on it if you're interested in learning more and going deeper, but understanding the four types of companies and identifying which type you fall under should provide you with a basic understanding and a foundation to start on, if you want to rethink your business model. It also provides a clear focus on what you should be focused on when it comes to growing your business in the future.

The four types are:
- Audience company
- Delivery company
- Infrastructure company
- Product Company

Audience company

This is a company that doesn't create or deliver anything. It's a *'middle-man'* business connecting the customer with their needs. Their sole focus should be building that customer network and strengthening customer relationships. A typical example of an audience company might be a finance broker, an insurance broker, a supermarket, or a travel agent.

Delivery company

The delivery company delivers whatever the customer needs. This is where most small businesses sit: Plumbers, Architects, Hotels, Wellness practices, etc. These companies should focus on increasing or improving the delivery experience and capacity. For example, a technical business might focus on increasing technical skills and capacity. A hotel might increase the number of guest rooms or other guest experiences.

Infrastructure company

The infrastructure company is the backbone of every other type of business, including Investment businesses, Transport, Software, Traditional infrastructure, and Property landlords.

Product company

The product company is the rarest of all the types. Still, in summary, it creates new products and experiences for the customer. These products are generally innovative and groundbreaking. It works with the other three types, pulling them together to develop industry-leading products and businesses. An example of this type of company is the Virgin Group. This is also what our own business does.

Product

The Product section of the IMPACT foundation™ focuses on improving the customer experience. Are they receiving the best experience possible when they interact with your business?

When we talk about a product, we're talking about that *'thing'* your customer buys, & everything that goes into that. It can be a physical product like a can of baked beans; a service, like painting a house; or an experience, like attending a music festival.

If you've ever watched *'Kitchen Nightmares'* with Gordon Ramsay, you'll notice he'll order a selection of dishes from the menu at the start of each show. This is because he wants to gauge how good the product is. In many cases, those restaurant owners naively believe their product is the best thing on the planet, and the problem must lay elsewhere in the business. It can be the same in your business.

This boils down to six core areas:
- Brand
- Product offerings
- Customer experience & quality
- Delivery efficiency & systems
- Marketing & Sales
- PR & reputation management

Brand

This comes down to more than just a company logo. Your brand is about how your customers see you, not the logo or fancy tagline. It's about how you act, delivering on your promises, and the things you don't say more than what you do.

In the restaurant example above, yes, it also visually connects your business. This might include the colour scheme, the images on the menu, the type of seating, staff uniforms, etc.

Imagine you turn up at a restaurant to get some lunch. Your waiter wears a white shirt. The bar person is wearing a Real Madrid football shirt, and a second waiter is wearing a string vest. Based on your first impressions, what does each of these individuals & their dress code say about that business?

Offerings

What product offerings does your business provide concerning what your target customers need? Can you add anything else to complement your existing range or help the customer's buying journey?

Customer experience & quality

What do your customers experience when they buy from you? How do you manage quality control in the business? How do you ensure every customer experiences the same standard & level of service every time, regardless of who they are, where they are, and when they buy?

Delivery efficiency & systems

Is your business delivering its products efficiently, or could you change things to provide the same quality in half the time? Could you reduce your production costs?

Do you have systems and procedures in place, or are you employing excess staff doing things manually instead of using software?

Marketing & sales

You could have the best product in the world, but your business is dead if your target customers don't know about it. How do you maintain that customer relationship with your existing customers to keep them returning? What is your unique offer & pricing strategy?

PR & reputation management

There's nothing better than having other people talk about your business. It can bring people to the company you might never have accessed through traditional marketing methods. But the opposite can also be just as extreme. If a customer has a bad experience with your business, they might tell the world about it. How do you manage that to prevent it from ruining your reputation in the long term?

By considering all six core areas, & managing each proactively, you can build a strong foundation in this area of the business.

Case study: National hotel group

In the early 2000s, a small regional hotel group operating 13 hotels decided to go through what can only be described as a hockey stick growth program.

I came into contact with this group when they acquired one of our clients as they were nearing the end of their growth program.

Within three years, this group grew from owning 13 hotels to buying 835 hotels, inns, and pubs across the UK. During that time, they'd become the 11th largest hotel company in the UK and the fastest-growing hotel and leisure group. This is an impressive achievement. The problem is that their foundations were built on sand.

Every time the business acquired a new location, they'd divide it into two separate companies: a property company that owned the building and the hotel operator. The hotel operator then rented the buildings from the property company.

Both of these companies were valued differently. While the hotel operator might be valued at a 3x profit multiple, the property company might be valued at 10x its revenue. They used this same cookie-cutter model for every acquisition.

They'd buy an existing group of hotels or pubs at, say, a 3x profit multiple and split it up into two companies. The operating business would sign a guaranteed rental agreement for the property that was far more than the market rate. Then, the property company would refinance its business at 10x this increased rental figure. This gave them the money they needed to go after the next acquisition. Using valuation arbitrage was quite an intelligent model on the face of it.

Suppose they placed a rental figure of £100k on the operating business. In that case, this might reduce the profit and, subsequently, the value of the operating company by £300k. Still, it would create a property value of £1m, thus conjuring £700k, just by moving numbers around. They could then pull most of that money from the property company and go again. But here's where it started to unwind.

While growing quickly, they started to take on any business they could get their hands on to keep that hamster wheel spinning at the same pace. The thirst for that *'free money'* became uncontrollable. Over the three years, many of the companies they acquired were falling apart. Many of the properties needed a complete renovation. The problem was that the group didn't have the capital to renovate 835 properties; they drained as much equity from each business as possible to fund the next transaction. The operating businesses were underwater and forced to pay excessive rents, whilst the property company now had a large debt service to cover.

As the buildings were in such a poor state of repair, maintenance budgets had been slashed, and customers stopped coming. Many of those customers were coach tours, so the cancellation by a single coach operator meant an entire group of hotels would be empty for more than a week at a time. On a countrywide basis, that meant lots of empty hotels.

The business could no longer meet its debt obligations & the whole empire crumbled. Had the company used some of that refinancing to renovate each property, they would have kept their stream of clients. This would have created slower growth, but the balance sheet would have been more robust and the business model more sustainable. Unfortunately, their growth model was floored; they tried to squeeze too much money from every transaction, ultimately leading to its collapse. The lack of paying customers only sped up the inevitable outcome.

Asset protection

The next stage in the IMPACT Foundation™ is to consider asset protection. In simple terms, this means protecting what you've already got.

Whilst there are several strategies you can use, from an Asset Protection perspective, we'll talk specifically about the three key areas that most business owners dismiss but are the easiest to implement.

These are:

- Risk management
- Financial controls
- Diversification

Risk management

Risk management, in its simplest form, is planning for every eventuality, identifying potential hazards, and taking steps to reduce the impact on the business should an event occur. Another term for this is business continuity planning.

Imagine every scenario, from the business owner being injured and unable to work, or a fire in your premises. The first step is to identify why that event might happen and what actions you can take to reduce the likelihood of it happening or to reduce the impact on the business if it were to happen.

Example.

Scenario:

- The two owners of the business were involved in a severe car accident. They have been unable to run the company for four months. The business relies on them; they control everything that happens daily, control all finances, and are the only people with contact with clients.

Normal outcome:

- The business cannot operate, staff cannot deliver to clients, clients move elsewhere, staff and suppliers are not paid, and the company becomes insolvent.

Risk actions:

- Allocating responsibility to other persons, internally or externally, to the business.
- Have key person insurance
- Have key persons travel in separate vehicles on *'high-risk'* days

These are just a few of the actions you might choose to reduce the impact on the business.

After imagining the event, go into *'Day One Mode'*. What would happen? Who would be responsible? What if that responsible person was unavailable? Who then?

After identifying the events, planning what would happen, and allocating responsibility, it's time to train those individuals in a simulated event. When the simulated event is performed, and everyone feels comfortable with their responsibilities, it's time to test the theory. Throw in a few curve balls for good measure.

Simulate the event happening as if it were real. Switch off the power, cut the internet, disconnect the phone system, what happens? Don't tell those involved it's a test; just let them get on with it and see how they cope. You don't need to do a full simulation. You obviously wouldn't set a fire in your office. Still, when your staff arrive at work in the morning, you could lock the entrance door and tell them there's been a fire and no access is available. Those emergency procedures should kick in straight away.

From this practice drill, you'll see how people react under pressure. You'll see some crumble whilst others step up. Those who step up, you know, are the ones who can lead the business. You'll also spot gaps in the training and opportunities for improvement. It'll help each staff member improve their problem-solving skills, if nothing else.

In addition to the obvious business continuity reason behind doing this, there's an element of legal responsibility on the business owner's part. In the event something did happen, perhaps causing injury or damage to another person.

If you discovered that you'd not trained staff or taken precautions, testing various scenarios, you could be held personally liable for breaching your responsibilities.

There's also the issue of another company being damaged by an event, such as a client being impacted by a revenue loss or incurring higher costs. They may have a legal claim against your business. This can be as simple as them suffering a delay to a contract (such as a construction project) or a disruption of service availability.

Managing Risk also connects us seamlessly to our next area of focus, Diversification.

Diversification

Suppose your biggest client makes up 40% of your monthly or annual revenue. What would happen to your business if something happened to that client?

I've asked this to many business owners who rely on a large portion of their business from corporate clients. The consensus among all these people is that such a large client will not go bankrupt. People have very short memories in this respect, and things always seem rosy when the sun is shining. The mind will always find evidence to back up its assumptions; this is called confirmation bias, and it's hazardous if you're not dealing with facts.

We often see large, high-profile corporate insolvencies as anomalies, a unicorn in the market, something that will never happen to our client. This comes from an emotional standpoint; they're so in awe of winning that large client that they're blind to seeing the fundamentals behind that client's business. In many cases, if we spend just a few minutes doing some research, we might see lots of red flags for that client - profit warnings, high levels of debt, court cases with suppliers, restructuring, finance directors resigning, making a loss on contracts, poor liquidity ratios, poor credit scores. If those same red flags were present in a small local business, would you be so keen to work for them?

The sad fact is that if something happens with these clients, many small businesses won't be able to recover. Is that blind naivety worth losing everything you've built? It doesn't need to be this way. If we're willing to be honest with ourselves, remove the emotional bias, stop the hero-worshipping bullshit, and start to look at the fundamentals.

If I were to tell you that your 40% client had an 87% chance of going insolvent in the next three years, would you be so keen to continue as you are, or would you prefer to do things differently, putting in place some actions to reduce that impact should it occur?

Sector diversification

We aren't just concerned with client concentration, however. The same diversification principle applies to sectors. While sector diversification has a longer-term focus than client diversification, sector risk typically involves longer cycles, such as an economic cycle.

When the economy goes into recession, the construction industry is usually one of the first casualties. Customers cannot afford to borrow for new buildings, so construction demand drops. If 50% of your clients are in the construction industry, 50% of your business will be impacted when this happens. By diversifying across multiple sectors, the impact on your business won't be as severe if one industry is hit.

Supplier diversification

The last area is supplier diversification. It is less important than client or sector diversification. Still, it needs some attention, especially if your business model relies on suppliers.

If you rely on one supplier, whether a service provider or a manufacturer, how will your business be able to continue if something happens to that supplier? That doesn't necessarily mean they go insolvent; it could just mean experiencing problems. Would you still be able to operate your business? What would the timescale and likely costs be to transfer to other suppliers?

The other issue with supplier diversification is that if you're reliant on a single supplier and that supplier reduces your credit terms, they can dictate whether your business lives or dies.

Financial controls

How do you control what happens in a business if you don't have a set of financial controls or guidelines by which to work? It's okay when the owner is working in the business. Still, when you introduce staff to the equation, you need some financial controls. The obvious example is when a staff member buys from a supplier because they need something to do their job, whether a ream of paper or a piece of equipment. Without controls, anyone can purchase on behalf of the company, leaving you, as the business owner, to pay for it.

When there are no financial controls, a staff member will generally go to either the big name brand or someone they know, a friend or relative, rather than the supplier with whom you've already negotiated the best discounts and credit terms. I've even witnessed ex-employees of a business go into a supplier & buy equipment, buy it on the company's account, & leave the business to pay for it. Whilst you could consider that theft, it wouldn't have happened if there were controls in place.

But this isn't just about purchasing controls. Who dictates the largest contract you'll take on, and with whom? Is there an approval process for large quotes or tenders? Whilst a £1 Million contract would look good to some people, it could be the last nail in your coffin if you don't have sufficient resources to deliver it or the capital to cash flow it.

Then there's signing authority. Who has signing authority for purchasing, & are there levels by which a second person must also agree? I know of one business which employed about eight staff at the time. The business owner had health issues and let the bookkeeper take care of the office. This person had worked for him since leaving school, some 30 years earlier, so he believed he could trust her. However, it turned out not to be the case. Over a year, she embezzled many thousands from the business, creating fake supplier invoices, approving them for payment herself, and then paying herself the money. They only discovered the problem when the company was struggling for cash, & they identified that the business was on the verge of insolvency. Of course, she'd absconded by this point.

Case study: National construction company

Rok was a national construction company with its headquarters in Exeter, UK. Its tagline was *'The Nation's Local Builder'*, emphasizing regional subsidiaries delivering construction services under the Rok umbrella. The company started in 1939 as a local construction company delivering contracts to the public sector. After rebranding in 2001, it started a national growth drive, acquiring companies across the UK in Construction, mechanical, and electrical services.

Their strategy was to acquire established regional players in every city across the country; this meant that they grew from £43m in 1999 to £968m at their peak in 2008, employing over 4,000 staff nationwide.

Apart from their primary acquisition strategy, they operated a second strategy of underbidding contracts, essentially buying contracts, to remove competitors from the local market. While they were successful to a degree, they didn't have the financial resources to do this nationwide. Buying contracts, in simple terms, meant they were doing the work for free (or less than cost) and basically paying the client for the privilege of letting them deliver.

Such a strategy may have worked on a local scale, undercutting competitors with the aim of either buying them up or forcing them out of the market, but to do that on a nationwide scale was a bit of a crazy strategy; there were just too many competitors to compete against, some with much deeper pockets.

In November 2010, the company went into administration, owing subcontractors almost £300 million. The recession hit, causing a massive reduction in client spending. Hence, those contracts where it was previously making a profit slowly evaporated, resulting in a 30% drop in revenue and a deep hole in the balance sheet.

Cash

The fifth section of the IMPACT Foundation™ is about getting cash in the bank. It sounds obvious, yet over 80% of small businesses share this problem.

The sole reason a business will fail is that it runs out of money. If you give it unlimited funds, it will keep trading despite how good the business model is or what external factors impact it.

There are five key reasons a business will run out of cash:

1. Lack of profit -price wars, one bad contract
2. Illiquid assets - Stock, W.I.P, property, product development
3. Overtrading - Too much growth too quickly
4. Too much debt
5. Bad management - credit control, diversification

Hopefully, throughout this book, you will learn multiple strategies to overcome these issues. My intention is to highlight the potential problems; reading them should set alarm bells ringing so you can take the necessary action.

Cash flow forecasting

One of the first things a business should have is a cash flow forecast. This gives everyone a clear picture of what's happening and identifies any black holes in the bank account. Sharing this information with all staff will help them see how their decisions and actions impact the business.

It's surprising how many people view this concept as common sense, yet the majority never implement it.

Working capital cycle

Do you know your working capital cycle and how you might reduce the amount of cash the business needs to trade effectively? Could you change your business model to reduce the working capital you need?

In specific industries, particularly construction, firms like to take on as many contracts as possible but take forever to complete them. I don't know if this originates from a fear that they'll run out of work or something else. What this means, though, is that it takes much longer before they can fully invoice for their work. They have vast amounts of unrealized capital sitting in their WIP, or *'work in progress'*. A few months ago, I was looking over a company that came to me looking for investment to fill the gap in their cash flow. This company had 120% of its previous year's revenue as *'work in progress'*, yet they'd only grown revenue by 5% from the previous year.

Depending on the motivation, some firms will wildly underestimate the value of this Work in Progress in their accounts, especially if it's valued by a project manager who needs to understand the valuation method fully or perhaps wants to present a different picture than what's reality. Work in progress is the same as stock; it's dead money until you're paid for it. Apart from having dead money sitting in the business, operating costs are associated with it that need to be financed, reducing your profit margins and draining cash unnecessarily from your bank account.

If you have ongoing contracts or clients that haven't been invoiced yet, work through them and dedicate resources to getting them advanced as fast as possible. Then, audit how Work in Progress is valued so that everyone is on the same page.

Credit control

If you're poor at converting work orders into cash, this is one area that you need to focus on. For many small business owners, this can be a significant source of frustration & much stress. The problem with chasing debts, which I've found from personal experience, is that sometimes the *'chaser'* is paid based on how long they spend chasing it.

If it takes them one day, they'll only be paid for one day; however, if it takes them five years, their fees will grow accordingly.

In my previous life, I've been involved in court cases that took, on average, 4-5 years to conclude, resulting in substantial legal fees for us to pay, irrespective of winning the case. This sometimes made the win irrelevant, as the legal fees were so high, and the time cost of money involved, with it taking so long to receive a settlement. I've since learnt there are much faster methods to gain payment that most of the *chaser* industry isn't open to sharing with you. It's these methods I adopt now.

But before we get to debt collection, there's a process every business should follow, which increases the likelihood of receiving payment before it reaches that stage.

1. Credit checking clients & allotting credit terms.
2. Signed purchase orders & contracts from authorized personnel
3. Identify the payment approval process
4. Identify authorized personnel for invoice approval
5. Taking an upfront form of payment (or security)
6. Interim or staged invoicing if more than one-month duration
7. Invoicing immediately after completion
8. Call the client - *'Invoice sent, did you receive it?'*
9. Two days before the due date - Call and ask if everything is on track for payment.
10. If not paid by 24 hours after the due date - Call to obtain the reason why
11. Every five days - Call & follow up with an email
12. Aim to get part payment - this reinforces their admittance of owing the debt.
13. If there is no progress, move to legal process.

14. Everything discussed on the phone is copied to email to maintain a paper trail.

This checklist comes from years of being burnt by people who believed they had a right to take something from us yet never pay for it. Here's just one example.

Case study: Credit control

Having worked for one particular client for a few years, mostly on much larger projects, we trusted him, so when it came to working on his own property, we naively relied on a handshake. We didn't ask for written orders, & we didn't sign contracts. Our only process was providing the client with a quote detailing the work we'd do, to which the client agreed. As far as we were concerned, we'd both get what we wanted. For him, a nicely renovated house, & for us payment on time. At the time, we were working on other, larger contracts with him, so we had no fear of not being paid. So we started work.

Four months after completing the work, the final invoice had been submitted, yet there was still no sign of payment. After many visits to his home to negotiate a settlement, the client refused to pay us any money. He argued that he wanted to avoid paying us the VAT on the invoice, & we either accept payment in cash, without the VAT, or he wouldn't pay anything at all. This wasn't an option, as we'd have been committing VAT fraud by doing that, so we were forced to start the legal proceedings.

The client's opening defence, which took around 12 months from first engaging a lawyer, was that the house did not belong to him. It was not registered in his name but in his father-in-law's name. From a legal perspective, this was no different from a random person down the street instructing us to do the work on the property. Our client refused to admit he had instructed the work & his father-in-law; whilst we knew him, he had never been to the property or had any dealings with the project, nor did he move into the property when it was complete; as such, refused any liability for the debt.

Until then, we'd mainly worked on larger commercial contracts such as hotels or government contracts, so checking the land registry was a new concept. Needless to say, we were more cautious from that point on. The entire process took four years to reach its conclusion. We won the case but didn't receive payment, as the client owned no assets. However, our lawyer still needed to be paid.

Team

The last section of our IMPACT Foundation™ is about you, the business owner, and the people you employ in the business.

We'll discuss this in two stages: the areas that lead to a decline and what happens when you're in that black hole.

So, what events lead to a business's decline from a people perspective? Many events could lead to a business's stagnation or decline, but we'll cover two of the most common.

Everyone wants to be the CEO

Some people won't like me saying this, but the most common theme is when a business owner steps into the wrong role in a business as if it's their birthright. I'm talking about when a heavily technical-biased person, who should be focused on delivery, instead tries to run the company. Two different skill sets & two very different personality types are needed for either role. This isn't even about having the right *'qualifications'*. It's a problem created by the ego, whether because a business owner wants to be seen by everyone as the *'owner'* or fear of losing control that causes a technical personality to step into the Managing Director or CEO role.

Let me explain why this is bad if it isn't apparent already. As a technical personality, you enjoy getting into the technical details of what you do, whether analyzing the numbers or building the house, and you're focused on TODAY. That's all that matters to you. Your natural programming is to think about today.

A leadership-based role, such as a CEO or managing director, regardless of what label you put on it, should be focused on the future and drive the business toward some future target. To achieve this, that individual has to have a *'dreamer'* personality, be creative, be a strategic thinker, and be focused on moving the big pieces instead of being tied up in detail. You cannot switch personality types; it's what you're born with. Over 70% of people are born into that *'technical'* category - The Do'er.

Often, when you have a technical personality running the company, the business won't grow. It'll grow a little at first, perhaps servicing the needs of close connections. Still, otherwise, it will generally just tick along, sometimes going through cycles of drought, where there isn't enough work for staff because rather than looking for new growth opportunities, the *'leader'* has defaulted to his natural position of focusing on the nuts & bolts of today, rather than winning that next contract, or moving that next strategic piece closer.

There's a reason why some companies seem to grow effortlessly, whilst others struggle to maintain their current status. It all comes down to people. A company is just a group of people who have come together to achieve a shared objective. The difference between achieving that objective and not is all about the people in the business, particularly having the right mix of these personality types.

The first thing to do is recognize the problem. A bruised ego is better than a failed business. If it makes you feel better, understand that when you get this right, your business will become much more successful—the difference will be like night and day. Over 80% of small businesses I've encountered share this same problem.

The solution is first to find someone who can stand in that role naturally, even if it's on a part-time basis. The leadership energy doesn't need to be active every day. It's not this person's job to manage staff or details. Its sole responsibility is to create a vision for the business and then choose & oversee several strategies to achieve that vision. If you're that technical personality, then you're responsible for delivering the product offering, such as ensuring quality standards are kept to a high standard, answering queries from staff or clients and making the delivery process as efficient as possible. Think of yourself as the technical expert in the business.

As a technical expert, if you were considering career development training, your focus should be improving your technical knowledge and skills rather than learning the usual, more generic management training. Ideally, you'll be the person customers look to when they need an answer to something technical.

Your new management team will include the following responsibilities:

- Leadership (future-focused, strategy & product creation)
- Operational management (organizing people)
- Commercial relationships (sales & marketing)
- Technical delivery
- Financial management

Suppose you're that technical personality, & your business doesn't have a full management team yet. In that case, you can fill a couple of the other management roles, depending on your skills & experience. Operational management needs good organizational skills, such as project management, and the ability to manage & motivate people. If you have a financial background, perhaps with some guidance, you could also temporarily fill the financial management role. Attention to detail is the skill set shared between both these roles. As the business grows, the focus should be on filling these roles individually, with strong candidates in each role.

Another example is a marketing company that, surprisingly, wasn't very good at marketing its own business. It was so focused on delivering marketing services to its clients (technical delivery) that it kept forgetting to find new clients for its own business.

Suppose you have all five of these roles covered. In that case, the focus shifts to identifying weaknesses or gaps in that team, possibly due to one individual's inexperience.

Aside from creating a management structure, the other concern is always about losing control & having someone else tell the business owner what to do. If this is your issue, it doesn't matter what position you play in the business; you are the shareholder. The shareholder has ultimate decision-making authority. The CEO is employed to act in the best interests of the shareholders. Being the CEO doesn't give them control over the shareholders. You won't lose control. A good CEO will sit down with the shareholders & formulate a future vision for the company, allocating responsibility to every individual in that management structure to achieve that vision.

Reputation loss

Loss of reputation typically happens when clients are unsatisfied with the experience they received from your business. One isolated occasion can be forgotten with an apology and a discount on the next purchase. If the customer experience continues to be poor, it becomes less *'forgettable'* even if you give the product for free.

Nine times out of ten, lousy customer experience comes from poor quality delivery, which, surprisingly enough, comes from needing a strong person in that technical role overseeing what is provided to clients. I've seen examples of when a weak technical manager is put in place, and the company seems to spiral out of control. Staff don't know where to look for answers, and eventually, they stop caring about their role in the business because they don't have that person they can look to for answers.

Suppose the technical manager has less experience than many of the delivery team. The delivery staff may see the business as a joke in that case. You often see this in family businesses, where a person is given a role in a business, especially at a senior level, not because of their ability but because of marriage. Staff only take the manager seriously once they've proven themselves.

The *'Up shit creek'* stage

So, after you've experienced the decline and the business is in trouble, a few things can be done, and we'll discuss a couple of them now.

While I discuss the distressed business here, these actions can be taken at any point in business life. Performing them in a company that isn't distressed will boost your results.

Too many cooks

There is a general unspoken rule that in many traditional service businesses, you'll have a ratio of non chargeable staff, versus chargeable staff. In other words, admin, back office & management staff versus those delivering the product experience to the client.

That ratio will vary, especially if you use automation and technology in the business. Still, generally, it is between 1:6 and 1:10, meaning you'll have one non-chargeable staff member for every 6-10 chargeable staff.

If you understand this ratio concept, you can measure your own company against this metric & whilst it won't be your defining guide for the business, it's a good benchmark to work from. Of course, your business can employ as many non-chargeable staff as it wants to, so long as the customer is willing to pay for them through an increased overhead markup, but the better the ratio is, the more efficient your company is, subsequently, the more profitable it is too.

A better ratio also means it's easier to adapt when things change, such as when the country experiences a recession.

Get rid of the deadwood

What does everyone do in the business? In most established companies, especially those that have grown above 10-15 staff, you'll typically find individuals who always *'look busy'*. At one point in their life with you, they probably were busy; they might have even been considered the backbone of your business, but at some point, things changed, and they slowly became *'comfortable'*.

Maybe they got bored, or perhaps they realized their role was starting to become redundant or irrelevant, so rather than moving on, they instead made themselves busy when, in fact, their productivity levels were tiny. Slowly, this type of person seems to merge into the background.

Then there are the progress blockers. These are the people who go behind your back to stop things from happening, often turning other staff in the business against your plans. They might be open about it, or they might do it quietly. I've seen people are more open about their thoughts when it comes to much larger organizations; it's almost like the individual feels they have a right to make their will known to the rest of the world and, better still, make it happen. I'm sure we've all met someone like this.

The last group of people I want to talk about is what I call the *'won't change crew'*. These people generally say they'll try new ways, but they continue in their old patterns when it comes time. I don't know if this is intentional or if they can't break the habit. I've worked with a few of these people over the years, and they never changed, regardless of what we said to them or even how they were incentivized.

Everyone is entitled to their opinions and beliefs, but when it comes to moving forward, they can either get on the bus or F**k off!

With each of these character types, there's an opportunity for you to liberate them. Help them find a world that is better suited to them. They'll be happier, & your business will be more productive. When these people are around, they suck the energy out of the company. It might be uncomfortable, especially if you've worked with them for a long time. Still, you must find your balls (metaphorically speaking), & let these people go.

Case study: National FM contractor

In February 2020, an insolvency practitioner approached me about a national Facilities Management contractor they were engaged with and asked whether I could turn the business around.

This company had been trading for about 30 years but had been acquired by a new owner and his wife about three years earlier. The company worked for many of the country's well-known brands, including the major supermarkets and other top high-street names.

When I started to look deeper at this business, the first problem I found was that the owner had no experience with the company or even the industry. He had no experience running a business. His qualification and previous role were solicitors, and his wife was a housewife. Given their lack of expertise, I struggled to understand why they'd bought the business.

The business had declined since the day they took over from its previous owner. The owner had no experience managing people or the commercial process of quoting for contracts. He didn't understand the technical delivery and, from what I could see, didn't understand business in general. He'd signed off on contracts that were losing money every time the client picked up the phone.

The other glaringly obvious problem was that it employed 46 engineers nationwide, but 18 staff members were also in the office managing them. For this industry, you'd aim to have about 1:6 non-chargeable versus chargeable staff. Still, in this business, the ratio was closer to 1:2. This was another example of the owner being out of his depth, adding more office staff to try and fill his lack of experience.

The final straw was discovering that the owner owned the office premises in a separate company. He charged the contracting business a considerable amount of money to rent the office. He was less interested in the contracting business and more interested in making passive income from the rental. That's fine if the contracting business is run correctly, but he needed to learn how to run a business in this case.

This is a classic example of having the wrong person running the business.

The improvement plan

Now that we've gone through the IMPACT Foundation™, we should have identified issues or areas that need improvement. It's time to combine what we've learned and create an improvement plan.

Areas to focus on are:

- Intelligence - Are there any immediate red flags we identified?
- Model - Is our Business model relevant today, & how might we improve it?
- Product - How can we improve the product experience?
- Asset protection - How can we protect what we've got?
- Cash - How can we improve that finance position for the business?
- Team - Do we have the right people in the business?

It doesn't matter whether you're in financial distress, looking for investment, or doing better than you've ever done before; this process should be performed periodically, always looking for areas of improvement. There's a Japanese term called *'Kaizen'*. It's a process of continual improvement, working on small things every day and, over time, achieving massive amounts of change in the business.

This ultimately comes down to people. People dislike change, how will you manage staff & get them to buy into and adopt your new ideas or ways of working? This will be a significant factor in whether your plan is successful.

Summary

Part One of the book examined the various building blocks needed to create a strong foundation.

We followed the IMPACT Foundation™ first, gathering intelligence and data about the business to understand what's happening and identify which steps we need to take to move forward in each area.

Next, we looked at how important the business model is to the future survival of the business.

In the product chapter, we examined how the product offering and customer experience can impact the business, both positively and negatively.

From the Product chapter, we moved on to the Asset chapter, where we discussed various strategies to protect what we already have, including implementing a client and sector diversification strategy.

In the Cash chapter, we focused solely on maximizing cash in the bank. In the Team chapter, we followed this by closely examining what makes up every successful business—the People.

In closing, in Part One, we finally examined what we needed to do, created a plan of action, and considered how we'd resource that plan.

Part Two

The growth stage

Introduction to the growth stage

In Part One, we created a strong foundation for your business. In Part Two, we will build on that and accelerate the company's growth, building Momentum and ultimately taking the business where you want it to go. We'll use what we learnt in the IMPACT Foundation™ to create a Roadmap for the company.

After creating the Roadmap, we'll work through the Ten C's Framework™. This is where we'll look at the remaining nine levels of the framework and start and develop the business from a strategic viewpoint. Each of these ten levels is designed to move your business forward exponentially. Working on these areas could easily double your business's size within 12 months.

The ten levels in the Ten C's Framework™ are broken down as follows:

- Compass - Understanding where you are now, & where you want to go
- Community - Covering the broader type of audience
- Club - Get on the radar of your ideal clients
- Credentials - Taking internal actions to build credibility with your ideal client
- Credibility - The steps you need to take to build credibility from an outsider's perspective
- Confidence - Closing the sale, & maximizing conversion rates

- Client - Selling more to your customer base without the emphasis on *'selling'*.
- Compensation - Increasing the difference between revenue & delivery costs
- Capital - Squeezing the most value from Operations
- Compound - The actual driver of wealth creation

Growing shareholder value

When we talk about growing a business, people generally think about it in two ways:

1. Increasing sales
2. Increasing profits

These are only two small levers in a much bigger machine. When considering growing a business, we need to measure shareholder value. It all boils down to this. It doesn't matter whether you wish to sell your business; every action you take in the company will either increase or reduce the value of those shares. When we're aware of this, we have a playbook by which to measure every strategy, & every action we take in the business. We call this playbook the Momentum Framework™.

To understand this concept fully, we first need to discuss the two primary levers determining your shares' value.

How much are your shares worth?

Business owners often ask me how much their business is worth. When I tell them the honest answer, they often feel disappointed. If you ask a small business owner how much they believe their business is worth, the most common answer is £1 million. The misconception of a business valuation, I think, has two origins. First is the media portrayal of the big Silicon Valley tech firms, companies like WhatsApp being purchased by Facebook for $19 Billion. People see this, & believe their own small plumbing business should carry a similar valuation. This is based on the psychological phenomenon called '*Anchoring*' - A large number anchors the mind, so numbers at the higher end of the value spectrum should be considered rather than lower.

The second reason is mainly with those unlucky few who have ever had the misfortune of contacting a business broker. See, the business broker model is incentivized to place as high a valuation on a business as they can feasibly get away with. They're paid a commission based on a percentage of the valuation, & normally, that fee is paid in advance. The sad case is that 98.7% of businesses listed with a broker never sell. But again, the anchoring principle works in this situation, too. For example, say two years ago, a broker listed your business for sale at £4 million. You received a few tyre kickers, but that's as far as it went.

Meanwhile, you were already off spending that £4 million in your mind: the new house, the emigration plans, the yacht, and the beachside holiday home. When a genuine buyer comes along two years later, they value the business based on its actual market value and other factors like how much of the purchase they can finance. They make you a more realistic offer of £950,000. You've already anchored the £4 million in your mind, and so you believe this actual buyer is just trying to hoodwink you. And so, you refuse the offer and forever lose the opportunity to sell your business. The worst thing about this situation is that most of those business owners actually end up closing the company down, & just liquidating the assets. They end up with a fraction of what they could have received had the business been appropriately valued initially.

I'm not interested in buying your business, and I'm not here to hoodwink you. I only intend to show you its actual market value so you can use it as the *'You are here'* marker on your Roadmap.

So, let's look at how the business is valued. The most common method of valuation is as follows:

$$Value = EBIT \times Multiple$$

There's another lever to consider here: debt on the balance sheet. We won't consider debt in this exam, but it's essential to consider it. Some industries, such as commercial property or software, replace the EBIT figure with revenue. Still, the overall valuation model is fundamentally the same.

If we know these are the levers, then we also know that to increase the value of the shares, we have to adjust each of those levers. How do we do that?

EBIT

EBIT is an accounting term used to describe profit in a business. It stands for *'Earnings Before Interest & Tax'*. From an actual measurement perspective, it's slightly different from net profit, but to keep this simple, let's just think of it as net profit. After adjusting the EBIT figure for the owner's salary & takings, replacing them with the market rate for our role in the business, we're left with a profit figure to base our valuation on. This is the first pillar in our valuation formula. We'll look at strategies to increase that figure later in the book.

The multiple

The choice of multiple is a controversial topic in many circles, so rather than talk about specific numbers based on records of companies that have sold. Instead, we'll talk about the factors which affect the multiple. These are:

- Scale
- Liquidity of your shares
- Economic conditions & timing
- Market Appetite
- Access to Finance

We can't control the last three. However, we can be aware of them, & make the right choices based on these three factors. Let's look at the other two, Scale & Liquidity, as these are the factors under our control.

Scale

There's a simple truth when it comes to scale. The larger a business is, the larger the multiple increases. Let me explain why. The primary reason is that smaller firms are considered more risky than larger businesses. In a small business, one client or one key member of staff can leave, & it can have a drastic effect on the company. Likewise, at the opposite end of the spectrum, if a manager leaves a large corporate firm, it will not impact that business's operating performance.

The second reason is all about where the money is. If you consider the pool of investment capital to be like an inverted pyramid, it's very shallow at the pointy end of that pyramid; there is little capital there. As you move to the other end of that pyramid, the larger that pyramid gets, the more capital available. Now, replace that pyramid with the business community. At the pointy end, these are the micro businesses in the economy. At the other end, this represents huge corporate firms.

The pool of investment capital is greater as you move through that pyramid. It's often said it's much easier to raise £100 million than raise £1 million. With this fact in mind, the fewer '*buyers*' there are, the less capital available. To look at this from a different viewpoint, the law of supply & demand dictates that increasing the number of potential buyers (increased demand) creates a bidding war and pushes the price up. If there are no buyers, demand is low, & so the price is dictated by whatever someone is willing to pay - In other words, the buyer dictates the price.

This all translates to the valuation formula. The multiple increase correlates to the size of the business. This happens at various levels, especially in the small business end of the market. I've shown the valuation multiples below as an example. Each industry & type of business varies. However, there's market research reports available that show the average multiple paid in each sector across hundreds of acquisitions globally. Here's an example of how scale relates to the multiple:

- < £1m revenue = x1 multiple
- < £2m revenue = x2 multiple
- < £5m revenue = x3 multiple
- < £10m revenue = x4 multiple
- < £25m revenue = x5 multiple
- < £100m revenue = x10 multiple

Now that we understand this correlation, we know that if we wish to increase the multiple, we must also increase the business size.

Share liquidity

As we saw with scale, the perceived risk level of an investment is also a significant factor in how much value is placed on a business by the market. Small companies are perceived as risky by the investment community. If an investor invests in a small business, it could be ten years before they see a return on their investment. The shares aren't liquid. There isn't a market where shares in a private company can be traded. They're essentially worthless unless an investor can find someone willing to buy those shares. The situation is much worse when the investor is a minority shareholder.

It always surprises me when a business owner fights over what percentage of equity they're willing to give away to investors or partners when, in reality, it doesn't matter. It's just imaginary numbers on a piece of paper. The chance of them achieving a sale of those shares is tiny. The investor understands this, and they're choosing to join you on a journey. It's less about becoming a billionaire and more about impacting your business, & having a new project to occupy their mind. Suppose you've ever watched programs like Dragons Den. In that case, many people who secure investments there, will never achieve a sale in the future. For the dragons, the most common way for them to exit is either to sell their shares back to the business owner, or integrate it into one of their other investments. The businesses don't grow large enough to attract that larger pool of capital.

Share liquidity might not bother you as a business owner. Still, it's a real issue for an investor with no emotional connection to the business. For this reason, it makes the multiple of a private company very low compared to the equivalent-sized public company.

A business with publicly traded shares on a leading stock exchange, like the Nasdaq or the London Stock Exchange, typically has shares valued at two or three times the value of an equivalent private company.

Having a publicly listed company means your shares are tradable and liquid; hence, they're now worth twice as much. As an investor, I can buy and sell my shares in a public company on the same day.

So, as with scale, if you wish to increase the multiple in the valuation formula, converting your private shares to liquid, tradable shares also increases that multiple.

The momentum value drivers

Now that we understand these are the drivers of value in a business, every choice we make, every strategy we choose, & every action we take should be directly connected to impacting one or more of these value drivers. Throughout the Momentum Framework™, we'll look at many strategies to achieve this.

Money in your pocket

The final thing we must consider before diving into the Momentum Framework™ is money in your pocket. It's all well and good to own a business, but if you're penalized for liquidating any of that value for personal use, then what's the point?

I'm talking here about how you structure the business to keep as much of that cash as possible. We're talking about this on two levels:

- Business taxation
- Personal taxation

Suppose your business can reduce its tax bill by 10% every year. In that case, that means you've got an extra 10% to invest in growing the business, employing more staff, & making the world a better place. You might even invest it in another company. A typical business owner doesn't *'squirrel away'* every penny into a drawer, saving it for a rainy day.

If you have extra money available, it's either invested into something else or used to fund some purchase, whether a new TV, a classic car, or a holiday home on the Riviera. So, every penny in tax savings goes straight back into the economy, one way or another.

Considering this argument, are the governments of the world a more efficient way of building an economy by increasing taxes, or would we be better placed to tax everyone less, & let the economy flourish? When a government taxes its citizens, it removes money from circulating in the economy. If I had more money, I would have much more to distribute to the world. I'll leave you to consider the debate for yourself.

In my book, *'Sustainable Community: A Framework for a Better Future'*, I go much deeper into the debate on taxes, and I present an alternative way for economies to flourish.

Which side of this debate you sit on will also depend on whether you consider strategies to reduce your tax liabilities. On a personal tax level, structuring your tax situation to minimize income tax, as well as capital gains & inheritance tax, not only helps you increase your lifestyle choices but also enables you to invest in other businesses, support local community projects, and most importantly it preserves your wealth for your future generations. This is how we remove poverty from the world.

Now, I won't share any tax reduction strategies with you. Everyone's tax status will be different, & there are much better experts than me available to help. My only intention is to shine a spotlight & make you aware of the opportunities. The next step is up to you.

Everything is an investment

I want to close this chapter with one final thought. It doesn't matter what you do in your business; everything is an investment. Everything can be viewed as an investment of time, money, resources, or shares.

So whether that's a new marketing campaign, buying shares in a company, creating a new product offering, or purchasing a franchise, everything should be measured to determine the cost of that investment versus the return you achieve from it.

Switching to this mindset repositions your way of thinking when making decisions. That includes decisions on how you spend your time. If you'd adopted this mindset, would you continue spending two hours a day talking to people on social media if it gives you no return on that investment of your time?

Maybe you would; it's your life, your choice, but again, I'm just shining a spotlight on those choices to shift you out of *'autopilot mode'*.

Your business is a vehicle for achieving everything you want in life. The only question now is, what do you want in life?

Case study: Training company

ABC Training provides various types of training services to corporate and government clients. It employs around 150 staff across the UK.

In 2018, their revenue was £9m, and their EBIT was £1.3m. The company had a valuation of £5.2m (£1.3m x 4 profit multiple). After some work to reduce costs in the business, the EBIT increased to £2.1m. Of course, the value of its shares meant nothing to the owner, as he didn't wish to sell them, yet he couldn't take any money off the table either.

After the profit improvement, the company was listed on a leading stock exchange with a valuation multiple of 9. This gave the business owners a valuation of £18.9m for their shares after listing, an increase of almost £14m.

Whilst the owner still runs the company, he doesn't ever need to worry about money again. He recently purchased a yacht costing in the region of £2m, which he borrowed against his public shares at a cost of £2,000 per month. Whilst he only planned to use the yacht for a few weeks every year, he volunteered the yacht to a private charter company, meaning it could be rented to charter guests the rest of the year, earning him sufficient funds to pay for the upkeep & maintenance, as well as pay off the loan.

In addition to buying a yacht, he also borrowed against his shares to invest in some residential housing projects, providing him with additional income streams & a potential capital uplift on his investment. None of these choices were available to this business owner until they switched their mindset of business value.

Note. Due to this company being a public company, the identifying details of this business have been changed.

The five stages of a small business

In the past, business owners have asked me what they should do to grow their business. Obviously, there isn't a blanket answer because every business is different, and you really need to be involved at a deep level to provide any impactful answer.

As it grows, there are many different levels in a business life cycle. You can think about it like climbing a ladder; at each step on that ladder, specific strategies or actions need to be taken to climb to the next rung.

We'll only cover the first five steps, as these cover 98.7% of businesses. Above those five steps, we're talking more about the corporate world.

Stage one

At Stage one, this is generally the self-employed person. It's the business that has one employee, normally the owner. In terms of revenue, it might have up to about £100,000 in revenue.

Strategies & Actions:
- Identify your ideal target customer, then determine who is already supplying to that type of customer.

- Team up with someone
- who already has a customer, then deliver to that customer, working through their business.
- Create a product offering that solves and delivers that customer problem so that your partner company makes money from the relationship.
- Consider the customer relationship a lifetime partnership, & treat it that way.
- Use a very basic level of systems to do what you need.

Stage two

Stage two is generally between 2 - 5 employees, up to £300,000 in revenue.

Strategies & Actions:
- Put together a team to deliver your product offering - Project teams

- Identify which products or services are in demand right now, & create product offerings around that demand
- Grow customer base through referrals
- Create case study examples & gain referrals & testimonials to demonstrate your delivery capability.
- Focus on delivering exceptional service. Generate repeat business from each customer.
- Create basic systems for tracking customer flow, & making things as simple as possible.
- Replace your unproductive time using external sources, such as software apps or virtual assistants.

Stage three

Stage three is between 5 and 20 staff and generally less than £2m revenue. This is the level at which most growth businesses climb and then don't go any further because the business owner is too busy trying to manage everything themselves.

Strategies & Actions:
- Build a management team to oversee Sales, Delivery & Operations, and Finance - Individuals more experienced than you in each discipline.
- Create a broad product mix where the customers can get everything they need from your business.
- Streamline the marketing & sales process.
- Create quality control procedures to maintain quality regardless of who or where the product is delivered.
- Create formal systems & procedures, training staff in those procedures
- Create a system for tracking finances in the business, including contract & customer profitability

Aim to remove yourself from working *'in'* the business so you can spend your time working *'on'* the business.

Stage four

Stage four is between 20 - 50 staff and typically less than £5m in revenue.

Strategies & Actions:
- Aim to remove yourself from the business completely
- Create a board, & attract someone who can lead the business without you being involved
- Build partnerships
- Cross-sell your products through your partners, & vice versa
- Create a clear focus on your customer experience, regardless of whether it's your business or your partner's business, delivering the product
- Create systems to manage the business remotely, using a dashboard to identify what's happening in each part of the business

Stage five

Stage five has more than 50 staff, generally up to 250 staff, and up to £25m in revenue. Now, only about 1.3% of businesses have reached this level.

Strategies & Actions:
- Attract resources, money & talent, leaving your team to grow the business day-to-day.
- Employ a professional team at the holding company level to oversee all businesses & investments, including a lawyer & accountant.
- Create a five-year product plan with the intention of having a full product range for all future customer needs.
- Acquire companies & other investments to complement what you already do or to reduce your existing operating costs.
- Customize the experience for each business stakeholder, including customers, partners, investors, staff, and the Community.

- Become a guardian & spokesperson for your industry
- Invest in world-class systems & tools that help you to grow & develop each of your businesses

There isn't really an upper limit on revenue or staff numbers in the stage four & five levels. At these stages, it's more about what you want the business to be, but I've put these numbers in because that's where you find that most businesses at these levels sit. Different industries & jurisdictions will vary; for example, a hotel business will have a different number of staff than a plumbing business at each level. Still, by reading each stage, you can identify where you are now and take the necessary steps for that stage.

Some of these numbers might merge into the level above or below them; this is just a general guide. You might have £500,000 in revenue but still need to use one of the strategies at Stage Two to move up to that next level, so as I go through each stage in more detail, think whether that's a piece you've already got or something you've already done in your own business, even if you believe you're at the level above. If you don't have a piece at one of the lower levels, it could mean your business might fall back to that level in the future because that's the weakest link in the business.

There's a clear focus or strategy at each of these stages for what is most important to you as a business and the one thing you're trying to increase—Cash flow, Profit, or Asset value.

So, for a stage one, two, or three business, your focus is on increasing cash flow. If you can get paid faster, you'll be more inclined to reduce your profit margins. An example of that is using factoring or invoice finance. You finance your invoice, which means you sacrifice Profit in the business because you have to pay that finance cost.

At stage four, you're probably sacrificing cash flow to improve your profit margins. While you charge higher prices than at the earlier stages of the business, you can also afford to give clients extended payment terms because cash flow is less critical at this stage.

At stage five, you're most interested in the asset value of the business, so you're looking at the business solely as an investment. You probably have a three-, five-, or ten-year plan with the idea of exiting that investment within that time frame, so your focus is on increasing the value of that investment.

Hopefully, by understanding these principles, you can identify which strategies best suit your business at its current stage as we move through the Momentum Framework™.

Level one: Compass

Now that we understand *'the rules of the game,'* it's time to consider where we want to go in life. Completing the Foundation steps in Part One probably highlighted a few areas of the business we'd like to improve. These should be considered during this phase of the process. The objective of this chapter is to create a roadmap taking you from where you are now to your future destination.

This phase generally focuses on a three-step process:

- Fix - Fix the problem areas
- Vision - What's the end destination
- Roadmap - How will you reach that end destination

Most people think the strategy is about doing things like Facebook ads. No, it's not. It's about big-picture activities. Creating a vision and Roadmap is about thinking about the '*big picture*' and looking at the various routes to reach that destination.

Fix - Fix the problem areas

Now that you've identified the areas you'd like to improve in the Foundation stage, we need to prioritize these according to importance. One method of assessing importance is according to their impact on the business.

Suppose you've identified something that might negatively impact your business, such as having one client make up 65% of your revenue. These should be the first things to work on in that case. For each item, you'll create a strategy to fix or develop that item. When you've identified the root cause, now it's time to determine what the *'good'* or *'healthy state'* would look like or what the desired end result should be, & follow that with at least one strategy to achieve it.

For all areas of your improvement plan, the strategies will most likely be based on completion timescales of less than 12 months. Depending on the severity of the item, you may wish to choose a much shorter time frame.

Fixing any foundational areas should be the priority before considering a future vision for the business. Still, as soon as these areas are strong, we can look where you want to go.

Vision - What's the end destination

I usually start this process by asking, '*What do you want your life to look like ten years from now?*'

Think about this across the six areas of life
- Career / Work life
- Relationship & Family
- Home environment
- Give back / Spiritual
- Health, Fitness & Wellbeing
- Finances

You can choose different categories, and some people choose more than six. It's up to you to do whatever works, to help you create that long-term vision for your life.

When you have a vision for one area of your life, how does that align with the other areas of your life? A helpful exercise is to imagine yourself living in that future state, how it might impact the different areas of your life, and what would need to happen for each location to support the others. For example, if your career vision is to be working 2 hours a week whilst the rest of the time sitting on a beach, that might align with your health & wellbeing vision but opposite to your vision for your finances.

When you've created your vision across all areas of your life, it's time to transition this vision to your business. Your business is a vehicle for achieving your personal vision.

What would your business need to look like to achieve the personal life vision? For example, suppose you need £10,000 a month in personal income. How much revenue or profit would your business need to support that personal income level? How many staff would the business need to employ from a revenue or profit perspective to achieve that? How many customers would the business need? How many locations would you need to operate from? Who would you need to manage the business? Break your whole vision down & build up the picture of your business required to achieve that vision. This becomes the long-term vision for your business. Ideally, you want to start with a timeframe of 5-10 years.

Now, it's time to break this long-term vision down into chunks. Go through the exercise again in a reduced timeframe. If your long-term vision timeframe was ten years, break this down to five years, three years, and one year. What would the business look like at each of these timeframes to meet that long-term vision? When you do this, as you get closer to the present day, consider what the business looks like currently. You might have calculated that past growth averaged 25% per year from the foundation stage. Consider that benchmark in your plans, but think about how that might grow by using other strategies we'll discuss later in this book. Here's an example.

Example.
- Current status: £1 million revenue. Ten staff. 25% annual growth
- Year 10 vision: £10 million revenue. 100 staff.

Let's break it down.
- Year 5 vision: £4 million revenue. 40 staff
- Year 3 vision: £2.5 million revenue. 30 staff
- Year 1 vision: £1.4 million revenue. 16 staff. 40% annual growth

After you've got a picture of the business for the first year, we can then break that down into four Quarters.

- Current status: £1 million revenue. Ten staff.
- Q4 vision: £1.4 million revenue. 16 staff.

Let's break it down.
- Q3 vision: £1.25 million revenue. 14 staff.
- Q2 vision: £1.15 million revenue. 12 staff.
- Q1 vision: £1.05 million revenue. 11 staff.

When breaking down the vision at each level, whilst I've only considered revenue & staff numbers in the example, it's essential to consider all pieces of the business for each level.

After identifying our Q1 vision for the business, we can see a difference between where we are now and where we wish to be in three months. Now, it's time to create a roadmap for the business.

The roadmap

At this stage, we're interested in three timeframes for the business vision: the next Quarter, one year, and three years. It's time to consider where we are currently and where the business will be in those three timeframes.

	Vision shortfall
Q1 vision shortfall	£50k revenue, One staff
Y1 vision shortfall	£400k revenue, Six staff
Y3 vision shortfall	£1.5m revenue, 20 staff

When we know the shortfall or difference between where we are and where we want to be, we must now choose strategies to achieve those numbers. We'll discuss some of those strategies as we go through the following chapters, so don't worry about this too much right now. You can come back to it later. Let's look at an example.

Example.

	Strategy	Budget
Q1 vision	Increase marketing budget & use marketing channels A, B, & C	£10,000
Y1 vision	Create new product offering, selling to existing customers	£50,000
Y3 vision	Acquire complementary business, with minimum £1m revenue	£450,000

Depending on the resources available in the business, we probably want to have between 3 and 5 strategies running at a time. This means that if one strategy fails to meet its objective, the business should still have grown through using the other strategies. This process is reviewed on a quarterly and annual basis, replacing each strategy with a new one as the objectives are achieved.

The second stage of creating the Roadmap is to think about the directions we're going to take along the way. To put this into perspective, if we know our destination is Rio, Brazil, our strategy is to fly by airplane. But there are some milestones we need to hit along that journey to know we're on the right course. So, let's look at what those milestones might be.

In our business, those milestones are normally measured in months. With each strategy, whether short-term or long-term, we should still hit certain milestones along the path. These should be specific and quantifiable milestones. Let's take a look at our earlier example.

Month 1	Milestone
Q1 strategy	Minimum 120 customer leads
Y1 strategy	Shortlist 3 suitable product offerings
Y3 strategy	Identify 500 suitable acquisitions

These milestones should be reviewed & planned monthly, with new milestones set each month.

After we've agreed on our milestones, we have to decide what actions we'll take during the month and, most importantly, who will be responsible for those actions. This process is typically planned & reviewed every week. If you can include a budget for each activity, that's even better. Let's break it down:

Week 1	Description	Budget	Who?
Q1 vision	Place advert in X magazine	275	TH
Y1 vision	Survey top 30 clients	50	BS
Y3 vision	Identify criteria for target acquisition	350	SF

It's important to consider, whilst, in our examples, these are primarily focused on growth-related activities, a few of your strategies might be focused on the supporting areas of the business, such as, for example, locating bigger office premises or recruiting & training staff. As you've broken the vision down at the quarterly level, there'll probably be many pieces that build that total picture. So, there'll be many more milestones and weekly actions needed to achieve each month's milestones.

It's essential that these milestones are reached across all areas of the business before progressing to the next milestone, or else those weaker areas of the company will drag the rest of the business backwards until they're also achieved.

Level two: Community

The second level in the Ten C's Framework™ is called Community. The objective of this stage in the process is to increase the number of new customers in the business. Compared to the rest of the framework, the Community stage is the most expensive & time-consuming method of growing the business. It covers the process of taking a fresh new potential customer, someone who doesn't know you & probably has never heard of your business, then attempting to convert them into a paying customer. This is where most small business owners focus their attention when trying to grow their business.

Some of the metrics you can use for this stage could be:
- New customers in the 'X' sector
- New customers in the 'Y' sector
- New customers in 'M' geography
- New customers in 'N' geography

These metrics will become more apparent to you as we journey through this stage in the framework. A few actions we can take at this stage help build the later stages.

Profiling your target clients

Following on from the *'Intelligence'* section in part one, you'll have already analyzed who your clients are, where they are, what size they are, and what sectors they belong to. Now, it's time to use that information. Starting with the largest sector first, focus on one industry at a time, taking it through each stage in the framework. Only after you've saturated all growth options for that sector can you move on to the next. We call this sector niching.

Let's use an example throughout this stage of the framework to demonstrate how it works for your own business. Suppose 40% of your clients are in the manufacturing industry. One option is to establish a sector niche targeting the manufacturing industry. Think of doing this as if you're establishing a dedicated standalone business serving just the manufacturing industry. This could be branded so that you're talking only to them.

Let's consider two examples.

Example 1: A Hotel Operator

You've identified that 40% of your customers are university students travelling during their gap year. You decide to set up a dedicated brand catering to this customer type. You create a brand name that speaks directly to this audience, *'Gap Year Travels'*. This new brand becomes part of a family of brands under your main company brand. Within the new niche brand, you decide to build out a suite of products tailored to this type of customer, including airport collection, tours, activities, & networking opportunities where they can mingle with other travellers just like them.

After you've completed this niche, you follow the same process to create a second niche brand tailored to your second largest type of customer: trades contractors. Within each niche, the objective over time is to further increase the number of customers within that niche, with the main target of each niche being large enough to operate as a standalone business.

Example 2: Architect practice

You've identified that 57% of your customers are in the Hospitality sector. Your main business is ABC Architecture. You decide to set up a dedicated brand focused on Hospitality customers, and you call it *'ABC Hospitality Design'*. This new brand offers a one-stop design solution for everything a hotel client needs when they want to design a new hotel.

After establishing the Hospitality niche, you copy the process for your second largest customer type, Social Housing. You create a second brand niche called *'ABC Social Housing Design'*. You continue to develop & grow both of these niche brands.

While you might think that doing this might alienate your other clients or potential clients, it won't because you'll use the same process for every sector. The best idea is to do this starting with your largest sector and working through to your smallest sector. This way, you'll probably cover 95% of your client base within the first three niches.

Go deeper - sub niching

We now take it much deeper. Within the manufacturing industry, there are many sub-sectors or sub-niches, so to be perceived as talking directly to them, we need to create something especially to suit each sub-niche. You may have discovered that 90% of your manufacturing clients come from the auto manufacturing sub-sector, whilst the remaining 10% come from a mix of aerospace and electrical appliance manufacturing so that you can position your branding around that. For each sub-niche, create a website, web page, stationary, etc., and talk only to them.

Profile your competitors

After creating your primary offering for each sub-niche, talking in their language, it's time to see who else is in the market. Who are you competing against for these exact target customers?

You might answer *'every other company on the planet'*, but that's too wide a net to cast. Only a few companies nationwide will target the same specific audience. Now, step into your customer's shoes. If you're a hotel operator looking for an architect to design a hotel, would you choose that architect who only designs hotels, or would you select the architect who designs social housing, house extensions, a library, council offices, or a care home? By positioning your business like this, you're perceived as being much more specialist, & with specialism; you're perceived to know more about your client's requirements - because you do it every day.

If you can identify those exact competitors, you can determine their positioning. What's their offer? What's their story? How are you different? Where do they rank in Google listings for your search keywords? The other benefit of being perceived as specialists is that people expect to pay more.

Now that you've got this information, you can tweak your positioning & fill the gaps where your competitors are weak.

Dedicated resource

The final point is dedicating resources to it. That means having someone responsible for marketing to that sector and running campaigns to attract new clients from those sub-sectors. It means dedicated advertising messages in dedicated campaigns by a dedicated person with a dedicated budget. It could be one person per sector or one person working in a different industry every day.

Dominating your sectors

Measuring how dominant you are in a sector is key to growing it. For every sub-sector, it's important to identify every target business within that sub-sector and your target geography. This is an excellent metric to motivate your team. You might locate 70 prospective customers. You can take this further by identifying who the business owners are, their decision-makers, the size of the company, & if it's easy to identify which competitor already supplies them.

Now that you've got this information, you can devise a plan to increase the number of clients in this field to 70. If you can identify a dominant competitor, identify a weakness in their business, & approach their clients, it could be easy pickings to help you do that.

You will never own 100% of a sub-sector, & the number of competitors in that sub-sector will determine how much of a potential holding there is for your business, but in an average market, having a 30% holding would probably make you a dominant player in that sub-sector.

Public sector

One sector I often get asked about is how to win government contracts. In the last 25+ years, I've bid on or overseen the bid process of close to £1 billion in government contracts across many industries, from renewable energy to software, financial services to fleet management. I've delivered contracts ranging from £50,000 to £3m each.

The good thing about public sector contracts is that you don't need to go through the same level of positioning as I've previously talked about in this chapter, including rebranding, etc. The key to winning a public contract is to demonstrate that you have the experience & competency. Setting up a brand positioning dedicated to the public sector would be beneficial to do this, though it's optional. The other benefit is limited competition - usually, there's only 3-4 firms for bidding each contract.

Contracts are typically awarded based on several factors, each receiving a weighted score. Price might make up 40% of the total score, with other factors like experience, quality management, qualifications, industry accreditations, and health and safety making up the remaining 60%.

While in some cases you may need to reduce your margins slightly to win a contract, it's one contract, one point of contact, one client, and one invoice. That one contract might be worth £300,000, giving your business guaranteed income for up to five years.

Growth by geography

Moving on from the work you did in the intelligence chapter, one thing you'd have learnt is where your clients are based. You may have discovered that some clients have multiple locations, some even in other parts of the country, and they're using suppliers similar to your business to meet their requirements in those areas. Expanding geographically could be an opportunity to service these existing clients further.

As well as growing new customer numbers by sector, another option is to grow them by geography, adding a new geography and selling to those chosen sectors and sub-niches within that new geography. It's the same marketing message: If you already have someone dedicated to that sub-sector, it makes good sense to give them a slightly bigger pond to fish from.

You can do this in two ways: virtual targeting and physical targeting. With virtual targeting, you can simply start targeting the wider geography; this option is easier if you can work remotely from your client and don't need a physical presence locally.

The physical targeting option means having a physical presence in the new geography. This is more relevant if you're delivering a physical product or service that can't be delivered remotely, like construction services.

It's essential to think about this, as you might search Google for a product or service in your area. For example, *'Gas boiler servicing in Wolverhampton'*. If you plan to expand geographically, it's essential to have a physical address & be visual in that area to your target.

That might mean having someone employed locally to go out & build relationships with your target clients. It might mean having an office address & local phone number that you can use for marketing or holding local meetings.

The problem with this growth route is that if you need a local delivery presence, it will be challenging to employ staff in that location until you have clients there. If this is your strategy, I'd encourage using it alongside the other methods we'll talk about in the book, as this is probably the most complex & riskiest strategy you can use to grow the business. It's like starting a new business in a new area when you have no connections, no friends, no suppliers, no staff, and no clients, but instead, just a constant drain on your existing business until you break even with your new location.

Dominate your geography

Before looking at a new geography, due to the high level of risk involved, I would first look at whether you're dominating your local geography. A focus on dominating your existing geography helps create a much bigger business, which can subsequently support & cash flow to other new locations in the future. It also helps spread local overhead, using any local staffing or premises.

If your business is very visual & you can dominate locally, for example, if you have a fleet of sign-written vehicles, opting to dominate locally means you might have 30 vehicles being seen locally versus if you have multiple locations, you might only have 2 or 3 vehicles in each area. How much more confident would your target clients be if they were bombarded with 30 vehicles versus occasionally seeing one vehicle every few weeks? It's much easier to be front of mind with your clients & target clients if they're constantly seeing your brand.

Strategy for geographic growth

Expanding on what you learnt in the sector stage earlier in the chapter, & what you learnt in the Intelligence chapter, a few pieces of information that help make a decision is to know where our clients are, including all sub offices & sites, not just their head office. If they are looking at geographic expansion, this could be beneficial knowledge, too. Plot on a map which service offerings each client buys and the GP% (Gross Profit Percentage) for each location. You may spot an opportunity to increase your profit margins by following a geographic strategy.

Using a mapping tool to examine clear patterns, you'll see where concentrations of clients are and where, if you set up a new location, it will improve those gross margins by reducing the cost of delivery. It might also show an opportunity to relocate your current location to better serve the market.

Exporting

An extreme version of using the geography strategy is to look at exporting overseas. When discussing exporting, people often think it's only possible with physical products such as food or machinery. Still, you can export almost anything, from digital products online to any service. The only difference between exporting and opening a new location in the UK is that there are different laws, taxation rules, and occasionally very different cultures to deal with.

If you don't have much competition for your offering locally, exporting is probably a good strategy. It'll likely be the same in other locations abroad, too. If you provide a more generic service, where there's lots of competition already, you'll probably have a high level of competition overseas, too, so it may be less beneficial to adopt the exporting strategy.

Client partnerships

One strategy to establish a new sector, geography, or both is to consider a client partnership. Within every area, you'll typically find a handful of dominant firms in each industry. Dominant firms that are probably, or could be, your client. I'm not talking about firms that provide the same service as you (though you could explore that avenue, too); I'm talking about your typical client, only much bigger.

If you want to open a new sector, let's say working for care home operators, there are probably independent operators and groups that might operate 30 care homes in your area. Setting up a partnership with one of these groups means you get a bulk amount of demand from day one. If it's a new location, with a key partnership like this, you're at break even from day one.

This is a strategy we've used several times. It won't happen immediately, but if you persevere, you'll find someone who buys into your plans. It might mean giving them access to a resource they need in a different way than they'd otherwise be able to access it. Would their existing provider offer that? Doing so could open the door for many more opportunities for you.

In any client partnership, you have to overdeliver for the duration of this arrangement. If they feel you're getting the upside and they aren't, it'll all be over.

Size matters

Often, when I first engage with a business, particularly at the smaller end of the scale, they'll ask me how to grow. The first thing I consider is who its clients are right now and what size those clients are.

Every customer has a ceiling on how much they can spend with you. In a B2B type business, if your clients are about the same size as your business, it will be challenging to grow your business. Consider the example of the corner shop versus the supermarket. The corner shop might sell ten tins of soup in a week. The supermarket sells more than that every hour. If you're the soup producer, your growth is limited by your customers' scale.

In a B2B service business, an excellent guide to use is to look for clients who are about 5-10 times the size of your own business. If you've got three staff, that would mean targeting firms with 15-30 staff. Think about this from your own experience of dealing with clients. Which clients impacted your business the most, and how did working with firms the same size or smaller, help you grow? They didn't help with growth. Some may have even been a stress for you and the business.

Case study: Media production company

In 2016, I was invited to help a production company grow its business. They'd tried a few things but needed more ideas, as nothing they tried seemed to work.

I originally met the owner, Sean, when I was looking for some public speaker training. After that initial interaction, Sean asked me if I'd help him grow the business. I have no experience in the Media Production industry, but I thought it might be interesting to look at anyway.

The basic business model was that their four staff would travel around the country, providing theatrical productions and pantomimes to various venues. They also provided actor training and a talent agency, but these were a tiny portion of the overall business.

The theatrical part of the business was losing money, while the other parts were keeping it afloat. The business model needed a complete overhaul. It was relevant in the 1970s and '80s but not in the 21st century. The clients didn't want to pay any more money, and there was limited demand for them, so the business had been stagnant for years.

By working with them, we decided to use a geographic expansion strategy. We repackaged their theatrical productions for the Asia Pacific market, a market with an increasingly wealthy middle class looking for traditional British entertainment and willing to pay very well for it. We established a local agent who proceeded to sell the production to a number of large venues across six of the main Chinese cities.

Our agreement was that we'd be paid in advance for our costs and then share the ticket proceeds with the venue. So even though we had to transport lots of equipment, scenery sets, costumes, 14 actors, and a production crew, all of our costs, including flights and accommodation, were covered. The entire opportunity was worth several million.

Level three: Club

The third level in the Ten C's Framework™ is Club. The objective at this level is to get on the radar of those new prospective clients you identified in the Community stage. This is where most business owners default when thinking about growing their business.

In the club

You first need to know where these prospects are to catch their interest. This is about knowing who your decision makers are, & which *'club'* they're in.

If your target clients are self-employed business owners under 45, there's at least a 50% chance you'll find them on social media. Over 45, you might find them more specifically in places more related to their interests. A friend of mine runs his own joinery business. He is 40 years old, and whilst he has social media profiles set up, he is hardly ever on them. But the place you're most likely to meet him is the local cycling club.

Some other places to consider your target decision-maker might be:

- Golf club
- Football / Rugby Supporters Club
- Motorsport / Car Club

- Charity
- Sailing club
- Flying Club
- Country clubs
- Networking groups
- Industry bodies

Integrating yourself into these groups, getting to know each member, & more importantly, becoming known to them could help your cause. To take it one step further, sponsoring an event & being part of the organizing team will elevate you much faster into becoming known by the members. When it comes to voluntary organizations & charities, I've met many high-profile people & business owners through being involved with them. Suppose you know your target client is interested in a particular cause. In that case, it will probably not hurt you to become a supporter of that same cause.

Trade shows & conferences

A trade show is an excellent way to be in the same room as your target audience. You'll find various opportunities, whether attending or speaking at their conference. Provide an educational 15 minutes where an audience can listen & ask questions.

You can exhibit and take a stand at the event. This is a place to start conversations and build rapport. One mistake people make is trying to sell to people, which scares them off. Nobody likes a hard sell. You can instead educate them, answer questions, and offer to catch up later with a free assessment or audit of their current business practices in relation to what you're offering.

The more advanced strategy here is hosting a trade show or conference event. Whilst this will be a big undertaking, if you have staff you can dedicate to the project, it will put you face-to-face with your target audience. You could even meet them as they come through the entrance to your event.

Awards events

As with the trade shows and conferences, there are industry award events that you can attend, apply for yourself, sponsor, or even host your own event.

Podcasting & video

Podcasting and video are the *'new media'*. In the future, they will be a viable alternative to traditional TV and radio broadcasting. Creating a podcast for your business could make you a voice of authority with your target audience. Perhaps interviewing other interesting people that your target audience is already interested in could also put you in their spotlight. This medium is becoming crowded though, so creating a unique theme or format would be beneficial.

Who are your customers?

Who already supplies to your target customers? Think of this like the food chain. Your business sits somewhere in that food chain. Who do your target clients buy from before, after, or parallel to you?

Let's say you sell cleaning products to businesses with their own premises. Many people in that food chain provide products or services to that same customer and may even influence what that customer buys from its suppliers.

There may be a cleaning company, maintenance company, bathroom & kitchen installers, architect, interior designer, or building materials manufacturer. If you're selling cleaning products, you're likely to buy from multiple manufacturers. They're below you in the food chain.

There will also be other products similar to yours that are purchased simultaneously; these are the parallel suppliers and could include toilet roll suppliers, stationery suppliers, catering suppliers, etc.

By mapping out where everyone sits, who buys from whom, and who influences the decision-maker on which products to buy, you can create a strategy to approach each party rather than selling directly to end users.

Partnerships

When you have your customer buying map, there are a few opportunities to move forward. The first is setting up partnerships with those companies you believe will benefit from offering your product to their clients. Consider how working with you might affect their business.

If they can increase sales without doing very much, there's a strong chance they'll do it. Then, it's a case of managing that relationship.

I've set up hundreds of partnerships in the past, and they take a lot of effort to maintain momentum. Ideally, you need to dedicate one member of staff just to keep driving that strategy and keeping people focused. Otherwise, from past experience, it tends to become a case of *'out of sight, out of mind'*, and the whole project falls over.

Client aggregators

A client aggregator is a business that groups your target clients together for some purpose. Normally, this is to increase buying discounts. There'll normally be at least one of these for every type of business. The only downside to these is that they tend to focus on price, so while you get access to the client through them, the margins will likely be lower, and some actually dictate what price will be paid.

How do your clients buy?

Everyone, whether you're a business or an individual, has a process for buying a product or service. Recently, I decided to try Reiki healing for a long-term pain I've suffered with my knees. It was a subject I didn't know much about or who to trust. I'm sure there are many charlatans out there offering their services without any form of healing ability or training whatsoever.

The first thing I did, which you might label as my *'buying process'*, was to look for a trade association or training body with a member directory. After identifying a handful of practitioners, I looked at their website; I was looking specifically for people who said they did exactly what I was looking for; more so, they had some external proof, other people saying it, through testimonials, etc. In other words, I was looking for a practitioner who had previously healed leg problems.

This was my buying process, and every buyer has one. They, too, have a process they follow to buy your product.

It's important that you find out what this process is. Some may advertise new contracts on their website, and some may have an approved supplier list that you need to register with. They may use specialist procurement portals, look at directory sites like trade associations, or outsource all procurement activity to a third party. The only way to know this is to ask them.

Managing performance

An important piece of any marketing strategy is determining which routes are creating the biggest impact on the business. We can become swept up in the euphoria of having a lot of noise and lots of enquiries from potential customers, only for those leads to go nowhere.

We can convince ourselves that such activity was a big success, & this is something I see with many people on social media. People write posts on Facebook; they receive 60 likes & comments, but that's it. None of that activity leads to an actual sale. They might have created a few like-minded friends, but that's all. You can't pay the mortgage with *'Likes'*.

When I talk about measuring performance, I mean measuring the number of sales each activity produced. This leads to what I believe is the best metric you can use for measuring performance: Client acquisition cost.

Client acquisition cost

By using the Client acquisition cost metric within your marketing strategy, you can judge which strategies are best based on results and, even more importantly, the cost of achieving those results. While one route might be ultra successful, if it costs you more than you'll ever get back in sales, well, it's not a very good strategy.

The simple structure of this metric is to take each route and calculate the total cost of using that route. Then, divide that total cost by the number of sales it resulted in. This would be the client acquisition cost for that particular route.

Example.

	Monthly cost	Monthly sales	Cost
Facebook Ads	1,000	10	100
Google Adwords	2,600	20	130

For example, if Facebook Ads cost you £1,000 per month, which results in 10 monthly sales, the Client Acquisition Cost for Facebook Ads would be £100 per client. Another way to look at this is when you know it costs £100 per client with Facebook Ads or £130 with Google Adwords to secure your clients, you can now offer a partner, say £90, for every successful client introduction. This may help incentivize them.

Suppose you know from the Client Acquisition Cost metric that it costs £100 per new client. That client probably needs to spend at least £ 2,000 with your business to recoup that marketing investment.

When calculating the Client Acquisition Cost, it's essential to factor in the cost of your time. Whether it's your own time or a member of staff, every marketing action you take will always involve labour in setting it up, managing it, and converting those leads into customers.

Case study: MOD client aggregator

If you've ever been to remote parts of Scotland or Wales, you'll have seen RAF fighter jets flying so close to the ground you wonder how they don't crash? Growing up in the Scottish Highlands, this was a daily occurrence, as we lived in an area where the fighter pilots would use the mountainous terrain to train for combat. With the first Iraq war ongoing at the time, it was normal to see three or four fighter jets in simulated dogfights with one another on the walk to school every morning.

The area was home to the Army and the Royal Marines, both of which had military training bases there. A few years after leaving school, we started to receive emergency callouts to both these military bases, normally due to power failure or a fault with their backup generator.

One of these emergency callouts later led to us replacing all of the lighting in the nine-story building, followed closely by a completely new commercial kitchen, all as part of an ongoing refurbishment and maintenance program.

At that point, we'd been involved in delivering various public sector contracts, but we'd never figured out how to crack the Ministry of Defense, and this had been our foot in that door, almost by accident. As we found out later, most of the MOD contracts are extremely large, generally in the range of £300 million. Hence, they are generally closed to smaller businesses.

These contracts are managed & delivered by either large outsourcing companies or defence contractors, who operate as client aggregators. The same defence contractor was responsible for every Ministry of Defence site across the region. This meant that by working with them, we could provide our services to the MOD without going through the formal tendering process, as is typical for government contracts.

Level four: Credentials

The fourth level in the Ten C's Framework™ is about creating credibility from an internal perspective. We'll examine the actions you can take, to create the perception of credibility within the areas you're in control of influencing.

This stage aims to create the perception of credibility in the minds of those businesses we'd identified in the Club stage, those interested in your product offering. Establishing credibility in the buyer's mind is essential to move to the next stage of the buying process. Without credibility, you'll go no further in the process.

Industry thought leader

One way of establishing credibility is to be perceived as an industry thought leader. This is about expressing your thoughts on the issues in your industry, offering insight & ideas on ways to improve, and becoming a spokesperson for the industry. You can do this in many ways: blogs, writing articles, distributing your thoughts via a mailing list, speaking at industry events, or recording regular videos on the subjects you're passionate about. Your chosen route is your preference; some are comfortable being on camera, while some are natural writers.

Qualifications, training & staff

Suppose you want a client to be confident in your ability to deliver. In that case, they might want to know about your training & experience. What makes you qualified to provide a solution to them?

You'll recall from the introduction section of this book that I gave you a rundown of the types of things I've been involved with throughout my career. Talking about the latest training event you're attending and showing certificates, builds credibility from a qualification perspective. Remember, though, it's not just you; it's Sally, it's John, it's Fred, & it's Debbie - it's everyone in your business. Suppose you only talk about your training. In that case, people will think you're the only person working in the company, which might create a negative perception of your business in terms of having the capacity to deliver.

Webinars, seminars & speaking events

Hosting an event where you can discuss ways to help your target audience is a great way to position yourself as an expert. This way, you also control the narrative. When you speak on stage, your status is elevated in your target's mind; they see you as that expert guide.

Book

Another way, similar to speaking on stage, is to write a book to establish credibility with your audience & communicate your ideas. It's a lengthy process to do it properly, typically 4-6 months of work, most of which is a full-time commitment on your part. After it's complete, you'll have a book to hand out to interested parties. If it takes your audience three hours to read it, that's three hours of talking to them, one-to-one, with no distractions. You have their undivided attention.

Videos

Video is the next best thing to being face-to-face with your target client.

Based on what I enjoy watching myself, the best videos are the ones that educate you in the process. In these bite-size training videos, you can demonstrate your expert knowledge.
Interview-style and conversational videos with lots of interaction are good, too. I'm less keen on watching a talking head for 10 minutes; I switch off mentally after a few minutes. I also like the walk-and-talk-style videos, but those might be a personal choice.

Branding

Branding is essential in how credible you appear to your target clients. Your brand is more than just your company name or logo. It's every touch point your client & target client comes into contact with your business. That means it's how you talk, how you dress, your daily actions, & even what type of vehicle you drive. Think of your brand like the sky; your logo is the sun, & the stars are every point your clients come in contact with your business - Your brand is what your clients see when they can't see the sun.

When thinking about branding, there are three different levels you should consider:
- Company brand
- Product brand
- Personal Brand

None of these sit in isolation; they all must be cohesive. Your branding will determine how you position your business in your target clients' eyes. Perception plays a big part in branding. As the saying goes, *'perception is reality*,' so you can make your business appear much larger or much smaller depending on what perception you want your targets to hold of you.

For larger clients, size creates confidence. For individual consumer buyers, size is less important than just being professional in how you do things. Let's imagine you set up a small farm shop in a remote village; if you tried to create the perception of a large corporation, your target clients would be turned off by it. In contrast, if you present your offering as the local farmer selling artisan food products, you could charge your target customers more than a large corporation could ever get away with. It's the same product, just a different way of positioning it, and your positioning starts with your branding.

The brand audit

A good practice is to start with a brand audit of the business, usually performed by an impartial third party. After starting with a clear picture of your brand message and agreeing on the perception you'd like to present to the outside world, the brand audit acts like a fresh pair of eyes, looking around your business to make sure you're creating that perception across all areas of the company and the customer experience.

Are all your vehicles washed, clean & tidy inside & in a good state of repair, or will I drive down the road & see them on the back of a breakdown truck, coated in 7 years worth of road grime?

Is your office regularly cleaned? I met with a cleaning company at their office a few years ago. When I arrived, I was led into their meeting room. The table & chairs were so dusty that I imagined someone must have been fighting with a bag of flour a few minutes earlier. It was apparent they hardly ever used this room. The irony is that this company provided cleaning services to its customers, and it would have taken them a few minutes every week to keep this room clean. Not a very good brand example; how many other clients have experienced this lack of awareness?

Are your signs hanging off the wall, or do you have letters missing on your premises or vehicle signage? You'd be surprised how common it is to notice things in your business but then get swallowed up in the day-to-day busyness. You forget you've seen it, and it blends into the background. That thing you should have fixed turns into everyday normal.

This all affects the perception of how credible your business is. The same applies to the overall state of your building. Is the building dilapidated & falling down, or is it a modern new build, well maintained, with a glass facade oozing with style? What message does it present about your business when someone looks at it?

Have you got a branded domain email address, or do you use generic email addresses like Yahoo, Hotmail, Gmail, or AOL? Using these generic email accounts subconsciously tells your target client it's just you working in the business.

If you're bidding for large contracts, there's less chance they'll take you seriously if they know it's only you working in the business. It doesn't matter if you believe you can deliver; it's all about perception, and that's all that matters.

The same rule applies to your company phone number. There are three types of company phone numbers, depending on how you want to be perceived. Suppose you're positioning your business as a national service provider without geographic boundaries. In that case, you should choose one of the non-geographic numbers (0800, 0845, etc.). Alternatively, you can use multiple geographic numbers to represent various operating locations (0141, 0121, 0208, etc.). If your business operates locally, the best number is the local geographic number; likewise, if you operate in two area codes, you could use the geographic number for each.

The third level of number is the mobile number. If your business provides personalized services, it's just you employed, let's say a mobile hairdresser, then it's probably okay to use a mobile number, so long as that's the perception you're trying to portray. If, however, you employ staff or intend to employ staff, and your clients perceive that you would need to employ staff to deliver what they need, then choosing a mobile number is the worst choice.

These choices aren't expensive. A branded email costs less than £5 a month, and most phone numbers can be purchased either as a one-off payment or rented for a few pounds every month. The next point is how you take calls. Answering the phone using a scripted message that everyone in the business follows, instantly elevates your company to professional status in your client's eyes. Suppose you don't have anyone to answer the phone. In that case, calls can either be diverted to your mobile without the caller knowing, or you can pay an external call answering service a small amount for every call they answer. With this external call-answering option, they'll typically provide you with a free geographic number as part of their service.

Staff branding

One route to improve perception, again, comes down to visual cues. This starts with uniforms, everyone wearing the same style of clothing. If interacting with clients, that uniform should be branded. Using staff ID cards, again, uniform & branded with the person's picture included. It doesn't cost much to set everyone up with a lanyard & ID card; you can buy the equipment & do it yourself or pay an external company to provide them, but doing so positions you as a professional in your operations.

What name do you give to the various roles in your business? Most businesses don't even think about this opportunity, simply just using the same as everyone else. But I've seen this for decades in the auto-repair industry and, more recently, in newer technology companies like Google. In the auto repair industry, you'll have a *'Junior Technician'* (apprentice), a *'Technician'* (Mechanic), a *'Senior Technician'* (Supervisor), and sometimes a *'Master Technician'* (Manager, Boss, Technical Director). Using a similar system in your business, just by changing a few words on a business card or ID badge, will reposition you in your client's mind.

Showcasing your experience

One of the best ways to create credibility is to show what you've done for other people in their industry. Creating case studies for every client, every sub-niche, every sector, every geography, & every product offering will help you cover all bases when potential clients start looking deeper at your business.

Case studies can be created in multiple formats: written, videos, press releases, LinkedIn posts, photos, etc. When making these, it's a good idea to create a basic template of the information you need to include in each case study and how that information will be presented, keeping a uniform appearance across the business.

Suppose you're delivering a project over a long period or working on a retainer basis. Creating a video/photo/written diary to update progress can be a good idea. An example of this, is when someone is building a house & posting updated videos & pictures every week to inform target clients. A good platform for doing this, other than normal social media channels, is Pinterest & Instagram, as people can look back over time, so if you've got examples of your past work, they'll see it as a time-lapse.

The same principle applies to any business. You don't have to be building a house. You could have a weekly photo or video with one of your clients, where you promote a different client every week. Suppose you prioritize just one of these activities and look to improve on it. In that case, this will have a massive impact on your business and on building that perception of credibility in your clients' minds.

Level five: Credibility

While the Credentials level focuses on what you can do internally to build credibility, level five concerns what other people say about you, while it's much harder to control, it has a more significant impact on increasing credibility for you and your business.

The objective of this stage in the Ten C's Framework™ is to gain as much external feedback & opinion about your business as possible. Doing this, further increases your credibility with target clients, naturally moving them through that sales cycle.

Referral

How many of your clients would be happy to tell others about you? Have you ever surveyed your clients to determine their thoughts about your business? Are they satisfied with you or just sticking around because they can't find a better alternative?

The first step in using referrals is understanding why they want to refer you to others. If people like what you do, even if they don't buy themselves, they'll promote your business.

I'm very interested in Resto-Mods. A Resto-mod is taking an old classic car and, rather than just restoring it to its original factory condition, treating the shell using modern methods to prevent corrosion, installing all the modern kit, a modern tuned engine and gearbox, modern brakes and suspension, comfy seats, and all the modern technology like SatNav and Apple CarPlay. It's a modern car that looks and feels like it was born in the 1960s.

I'll happily talk to anyone about the companies that build these resto-mod cars. I don't own one, but that doesn't mean I can't discuss the businesses that create them. I like what each of these resto-mod builders stands for. I've bought into their story, & I like the idea of having a classic-shaped car with the reliability, technology, & paintwork of something much newer. I'll promote them all, whether it's the *Alfaholics Guilia*, the *Singer 911*, or the *Cyan Volvo P1800*. I'm a fan.

If you get people to buy into your story, you'll also create fans for your business. A perfect example of this is the *Eddie Stobart* haulage business. They've made thousands of fans across the UK and Europe. They even had a TV series covering 53 episodes over seven series. When you have fans, this builds external validation for your business in the eyes of the customer.

There are thousands of other haulage companies, some much bigger than *Eddie Stobart*, but ask someone to name an iconic haulage company, & *Eddie Stobart* will be the name on everyone's lips. For that reason, they'll consistently be shortlisted by clients when it comes to haulage-related opportunities.

Accreditations

One route to external validation is obtaining accreditations with industry bodies. Suppose I'm looking for a particular service. In that case, an industry body is the first place I look when I don't know a supplier. So, being accredited by all industry bodies gives you credibility.

Expert affiliation

There usually are experts in the industry with whom you can have an affiliation. We've done this a couple of times, the first being in our contracting business when we established an affiliation with various equipment manufacturers. By doing this, we became specialists in installing & maintaining their equipment. Still, to the outside world, our target clients saw that we were affiliated with well-known, trusted manufacturers - something none of our competitors had.

Borrowed affiliation

Advancing from the expert affiliation is borrowed affiliation. This is when you take a well-known business or high-profile celebrity and 'borrow' their brand.

This is called brand endorsement or sometimes brand licensing. The licensor (the celebrity) gets to put their face on your business or product in return for a share of the revenue.

You might see this example on social media when a celebrity works with a high-profile brand like *Chanel*. The celebrity will wear the product in public, be photographed wearing it, and perhaps post lots of videos online talking about the product. In return, the company will pay the celebrity an endorsement fee.

Trading licenses

Does your service require a trading license? You'd be surprised at how many rogue scammers are out there. If you have a license to deliver your product or service, why not promote it to your target clients by putting it on your website? Distinguish yourself from the thousands of firms that don't do it. The same applies to insurance certificates; how many firms do you see online that show copies of their insurance certificates?

Awards

Have you ever won an industry award? You can often be 'nominated' for an award by applying for it yourself. Some companies specialize in applying for & winning awards for their clients. An award can be an excellent way to show your target clients some external validation.

Certification

When your business has a systemized process, it can often be certified against international standards. Numerous third-party certification bodies provide external validation for categories such as ISO 9000 Quality Management, ISO 14001 Environmental Management, OHSAS 18002 Health & Safety Management, and SafeContractor for Health & Safety. There are international certification standards for almost every type of business. Each one of these badges helps to add credibility to your business.

Borrowed trust

Did you know it's possible to piggyback on the trust & credibility that's already been built up by other people? I'm talking about brands that have been around for over a century.

The best part about this strategy is that you don't need to beg *Mercedes Benz* to endorse your business. This is called brand association, which subconsciously transfers company values and credibility from these big brands to yours.

You can do this in your business whenever you buy a new company vehicle. You can do it when you design your company logo, the layout of your website, or even the colours you use in your marketing. A warning, though: you might be borrowing trust from a company that doesn't reflect your values, so choose carefully.

For example, certain car manufacturers carry with them a particular image that they've built up over many years: '*Cheap & Cheerful*', '*Middle of the Road*', '*High-end luxury*', or perhaps the image that other people have created, such as the '*White Van Man*'. When it comes to choosing a vehicle, there are generally four categories.

Ask the marketing team at these car manufacturers; they'll tell you exactly why they choose the words, the font type, the colours they use, & the purpose behind it. The low end includes *Fiat*, *Kia*, and *Hyundai*. The middle-of-the-road cars are the *Fords*, *Vauxhalls*, *Peugeots*, & *Renault*. The upper-mid end is *BMW*, *Audi*, *Mercedes Benz*, *Volvo* & *Lexus*. At the same time, at the very top, this includes high-end brands like *Bentley*, *Maserati*, & *Aston Martin*. The same rule applies whether it's cars or vans.

Suppose your branding & positioning are based around a no-frills, low-cost example, but all your staff drive high-end S-Class Mercedes Benz cars. In that case, you're sending mixed messages to your clients, which reduces credibility with them at a subconscious level. The same applies to the style of font & colour palette you use in your logo & signage.

With every type of font & every colour, there is a subconscious connection to what it means. Think of the *McDonald's* golden arches, that comedy style, bubble font in their logo has been so ingrained into our brains, if you use that shade of red & yellow or that same font style in your logo, you'll get the same brand association, good or bad. Most of the time, people won't even know why they're attracted to one company over another. Imagine if you're an upmarket restaurant but accidentally use the same colour scheme in your logo as *McDonald's*. People will associate your business with fast food rather than Michelin-star fine dining.

By finding a major brand in your industry, & looking at how they use colour or font types, you can get an automatic brand association with them. I'm not telling you to copy their logo style or look like a subsidiary of theirs; I'm considering the font style, & how you can incorporate it in your logo to make that subconscious connection in your target clients' minds. This is how graphic designers work when they design logos or marketing material - they know which colours represent subconsciously the type of message they send to the client.

Public relations (PR)

A tremendous external validation method is to use PR to have the media, newspapers, magazines & TV talking about your business. Places to think about gaining PR exposure are local press, national press, TV, Radio, Magazines, and Industry publications both in your industry and that of your clients. It's a good idea to work with a PR agency that has connections & experience in each of these fields. Otherwise, it could become a full-time job building the right connections. A good PR agency already has these relationships in place.

Affiliation with training bodies

Another form of expert affiliation is affiliation with industry training bodies that deliver the training and determine the qualification standards.

Licensee or franchisee

Becoming the licensee of a brand means you'll be seen with the same credibility as the more prominent, well-established brand without having to do much work yourself. For example, if you purchased a *BMW* dealership franchise, people would see you as *BMW* rather than the small business behind it. In the hotel industry, companies like *Intercontinental Hotels* invest millions yearly in brand awareness for their *Holiday Inn, Crowne Plaza*, and *Staybridge Suites* franchise brands, so why not piggyback with them?

Board membership

Sitting on a board elevates your status when it comes to external credibility. People view you as good at what you do, or you wouldn't be in that role. This credibility will be elevated if you can do this in your industry or that of your target client.

Build your own board

When Non-Executive Directors sit on your company board, acting as advisors to the business, their credibility in the industry rubs off on your business. Again, this is borrowed credibility.

Video testimonials & reviews

Getting your clients' testimonials or reviews is another way to build external validation. Recording a short video testimonial or review creates even more power. It can be shared everywhere: on your website, on various social media channels and video hosting platforms like YouTube, and even in your newsletter to clients, reinforcing how good you are. Clients always feel special when you tell others about them; it's their five minutes of fame.

Written testimonials

There are numerous online platforms where customers can post written reviews about your business. Search online for what you offer, identify which review sites appear on the search listings' first or second page, and then prioritize your focus toward these.

It's worth searching for your company name online & seeing where your clients have already posted reviews. Whilst we're talking about expecting good reviews here, there's a chance you might have created an unhappy customer. Managing bad reviews is equally, if not more important, than getting good reviews. Suppose you have a terrible review, & you can't dispute it with the review platform. In that case, it's essential that you focus on strategies to reduce the impact of that review on your overall rating. Having a single review that rates your business as one star will show the world that your clients think you deliver a 1-star service. However, if you mix that with a five-star review, your average rating will suddenly be three stars. The more reviews you can add on these lower-scoring review platforms, the better your overall rating will be.

Suppose you want to boost your credibility. Why not go to a site called *Glassdoor* and have your employees write a review about your business as an employer? *Glassdoor* is focused on attracting staff rather than customers. However, when a customer searches for your company, that *Glassdoor* review will also appear in the search results.

Case study: Renewable energy company

How does a new start-up business with no track record, & no brand grow to become the largest industry player in less than two years?

This was the situation when I joined a new renewable energy company. They intended to supply biomass boilers to the market. When I joined the company, there were just three staff & they'd been trading for about two years. After a further two years, we'd built it to 44 staff, £5.6m in revenue, a £10m pipeline, and twice the size of its next rival.

How did we do it?

The first step was bringing in people with a track record. That's where I come in. While I didn't have direct experience with biomass boilers, I did have 15 years of experience growing an Electrical and mechanical services company. I also had many connections in the market.

The second step was to get our services accredited by various trade associations, including third-party certification bodies for quality management and safety. Our letterhead displayed seven or eight different accreditations.

The third step was to buy an exclusive license with a biomass boiler manufacturer. This meant that if any client wanted to purchase that boiler brand, they'd have to come through us. By investing in the license, we were the only company in the UK where a client could buy this brand of boiler at the time. More than anything, this gave us borrowed credibility, as we associated with a boiler manufacturer.

By combining this, redesigning the business model, and following an intense growth strategy, we were very quickly established as the leading company for biomass boilers, with contracts across the UK.

Level six: Confidence

The sixth level in the Ten C's Framework™ is called Confidence. At the basic root of all sales, it comes down to *ONE* thing: How confident is the customer in receiving their desired result from you? The objective at this stage is to improve your customers' confidence in you and deliver what they expect. We will talk about some of the levers you can pull, which could greatly impact your sales conversion rate.

Reducing barriers to purchasing

The first area we need to complain about is reducing barriers. I say '*complain about*' because I see examples of this daily with small businesses. Many small businesses make their potential customers jump through 101 hoops to buy from them.

On one occasion, I contacted an accountant, asking them how they work and the range of fees they charge. I asked some very general questions any new potential customers might want to know. I never received an answer to my queries, as they insisted on me sending them, god knows what, paperwork, bank statements, and passport ID before they were willing to speak further with me. Most of the time, I've found this practice originates from two common sources.

Firstly, it could be a belief that doing so makes the customer view them as more professional because they've added a stack of paperwork & red tape to the process. Bullshit!

The second reason a company creates these hurdles is because they've seen other companies do it, perhaps a former employer, & rather than putting themselves into the shoes of the customer, they put themselves into the role of the technician, & try to prove to the world, just how technically brilliant they are -at not selling! Most culprits believe that if their peers are doing it, they should also be doing it without ever asking why they need to. Agreed, specific steps must be taken when dealing with a new client, especially concerning money laundering regulations.

However, ask yourself, does this need to be done before the client even decides to work with me? It's the equivalent of making someone pack their suitcase, go to the airport, fuel up the plane, take their pilot's license exam, and buy a plane, before deciding if they want a holiday. I suggest removing the red tape until after they've signed the deal - people don't like bureaucracy.....or the people that create it.

Agree on expectations now

Another common problem is not telling a potential client what you will do or the outcome they'll receive. I witnessed this with a business I became involved with.

When I met them, they were submitting quotes to prospective clients. Still, the quote was so basic that they only included the date, the client's address, and then a figure, which was the expected price. After I became involved with them, I discovered the problem when I asked to see their template quoting document. They handed me a blank letterhead. After creating an actual template quoting document, we sent over a revised version of the quote to one of their clients, and the feedback we got was amazing. They told us they'd received five quotes back, & all of them were of a similar standard & layout to our original quote, so when we sent over the new version, stating precisely what the company would be doing, the terms of the contract, the expected duration of the project, our process for working & how the project would be managed, along with a detailed specification of the work, they said whilst the quote was more expensive, we also looked much more professional than the other firms tendering. Hence, we won the contract.

The template proposal presentation

Moving on from the above example, the next thing to consider is creating a template proposal document. With another company I consulted with, every new proposal they created, they would open a brand new Word document on their computer, & start writing from scratch. There wasn't a single proposal that looked the same.

Numerous people would get involved in writing proposals; each person would do what they thought was correct. There was no uniformity across any of them. Put two proposals side by side, & you wouldn't know they were from the same company. The font would be Arial 14pt on one, whilst Times New Roman 9pt on another. The date would be in a different position on the page across both versions. The client address on one would be in full BLOCK CAPITALS, whilst the other might only have the first letter of every line as a capital. It was a mess.

Reducing the next step

What could you do to reduce the next step for your target client? The idea is to bridge the chasm between zero and making a £200,000 commitment. How can you help them experience what they'll get on a micro level?

Two examples, the first being the auto industry. Before you buy a new car, the car dealership will often let you take the vehicle on a 48-hour test drive to see how you like it. By doing this, you experience what it's like to live with a car.

The second example is the housing market. When you buy a newly built house from one of the national housebuilders, they'll already have a completed house on the estate, which they'll use as a showhome. In the showhome, they'll have all the best furnishings. They'll have the latest chrome fixtures, chandeliers, lovely stone floors, soft furnishings & best-quality kitchen units. They want you to imagine yourself living there when you step inside that house. This bridges the gap & makes you confident in making that sizeable financial commitment.

Another way to do this in other types of business without a physical product is to offer a trial period; for example, you might offer a seven-day or one-month trial. I've seen cleaning companies provide cleaning services with a period where the client doesn't pay anything; the service is set up from day one as a full client; if they aren't happy within that period, they don't pay anything & the contract is destroyed, but if they're satisfied with the service provided, everything continues & the company pays for the remainder of the agreement as usual.

Guarantees & risk reversal

What guarantees do you offer your clients? Do you advertise these guarantees? Every type of business should offer some form of guarantee to their clients.

Our contracting business offered all our clients a ten-year unconditional labour & five-year parts warranty on any new installation. If anything went wrong with what we'd installed, we'd fix it free of charge. Of course, doing this meant we also had a relationship with the building for the next ten years, offering additional upgrades or maintenance services. Offering a guarantee places your neck on the chopping board rather than your clients, and they like that.

The same thing applies to risk reversal. What results do your clients expect from you? Is it a 20% tax saving on their tax bill? What might go wrong in the eyes of your client? With no risk reversal, the risk is on the client's shoulders. They might pay you, but still not receive their desired benefit. By offering a risk reversal, it moves the risk from them & places it onto you. If you're confident in your ability to deliver, it's not a risk on your part.

An accountant, for example, might guarantee they'll reduce a client's tax bills to less than 10% of revenue. If they fail to achieve this target, the client won't pay anything for the work provided. If you're confident in your ability to do what you say you can, then making bold claims won't be a risk at all for your business.

Target the existing pain

Sometimes, pitching your client an exciting future state or pleasure is easy. I'm guilty of doing this myself; this book talks a lot about the future, & I've had to rein it in a bit. A better way, proven by the leading psychology experts in the world, is to target the existing pain with a solution to fix that pain. What is your pain right now? Bad cashflow? Cheaper competitors? Need more customers? I hope this book helps you start fixing that pain.

Payment plans

Rather than treating your client as a single one-off invoice, treat them as multiple payments spread over time. People will often be more comfortable spending £1,000 a month instead of £30,000 in one go. If they're only spending £1,000, they'll be more likely to find other ways to increase that monthly spend.

A side benefit of using payment plans is that you increase your profits without the client noticing. By helping them with the capital financing, they expect to pay a little bit more. Creating a payment plan enables you to create a steady stream of recurring income for the business.

Yes doctor

When a prospect comes knocking, they usually have a problem they must fix. If you have an irritating health issue, you go to the doctor. The doctor asks about the problem and then questions you about the symptoms you're experiencing. From this, the doctor can diagnose the problem and prescribe the medicine to fix it.

Most people wouldn't trust anyone like they trust their doctor. That's because they're seen by most as being trusted, educated, having the knowledge, and qualified to diagnose the problem, & finally, they're confident in prescribing the solution. Have you ever met a doctor that *'ermms'* & *'arrrs'* saying, *'I think it might be this, but I'm not sure, it might also be this too'*? No, they're clear about prescribing the solution in a very *'matter-of-fact'* way, and they're confident it'll fix the problem. Following the same process with your clients will have the same effect.

Pitching

How many people reading this book could say they've had professional training with pitching to a client? How many have heard of the elevator pitch?

Getting some professional pitch training for anyone in a client-facing role will help you increase conversion rates.

Presentation skills & speaker training

Are you confident in delivering a presentation to a group of people? Have you ever received formal training in the art of giving a presentation? How about communicating as a speaker? When delivering a presentation, many people rely on what the slides say and read it off, word for word. It's boring and disengaging! By having professional coaching, you'll learn how to do it and engage those you're talking to, motivating them to take the actions you want.

Get the right salesperson

There are two types of salespeople. The first type is the *'cold sellers'*. These people can sell comfortably without any prior contact. A typical example of this is the cold caller stereotype. The good ones can build instant rapport with people.

The second type is the longer-term relationship builders. In a way, both these types are opposite in how they operate. The relationship builder will often struggle to sell without having built up that relationship over time. Still, as time passes, they'll increase their sales results at every interaction. In most cases, the *'relationship builder'* will far outsell the 'cold seller' over the long term.

I discovered my preference when I worked alongside someone who was the cold seller type. I'm more of a relationship builder. It feels unnatural, & forced if I try to sell someone at the first point of contact. Putting the cold seller type into a relationship builder role has the opposite effect; they're always trying to sell at every opportunity, so the client views them as less trustworthy, and the relationship breaks down. The ideal scenario is to have both types in the business.

You have someone to open the conversation & build initial rapport, then someone to take over & manage that relationship, usually the account manager or relationship manager role.

Sales training

When was the last time your staff received professional sales training? Unless your business is a sales agency, your staff probably receives very little sales training. Having your staff undergo a sales training program can help get everyone on the same page and improve conversion rates.

Building the relationship

What are you doing to build that customer relationship? How are you staying on their radar so they won't forget you? Have you ever noticed that when a friend asks if you know someone who provides *'XYZ services'*, you can instantly think of certain people? I usually think of at least one person within my network.

But my point is that I have more than one suitable person in my network. I have 147 people who would fit the opportunity. So why do one or two people stand out in my mind, yet the other 145 don't?

An unspoken rule in sales and marketing circles says you need to give someone 12 points of value to stick in their mind. That means giving people something that adds value to their lives and doing it at least 12 times before you can expect them to think of you and become front of mind.

As an apprentice, I remember one project where we installed a new heating system in someone's house. The customer was the parents of one of our competitors, which makes this story stand out in my memory even more. When we talked to the customer one evening, just before heading home, she said she loved these sweets called '*Ginger Toffees*'. They were hard to find, and her friend had just brought her some back from Australia. Hence, it was an exciting occasion for her to receive them.

By chance, my Mum at the time, unknown to our customers, worked in a confectionary factory, making various types of sweets. One of the sweets they made was Ginger Toffees. So, on the last day of the project, we took the customer a box of ginger toffees. She was over the moon.

About two years later, her neighbour called to request we work on a new house they were building. Our original customer had recommended us for the project. Sometime after that, I bumped into them on the high street. I didn't recognize them, but they were just as happy to see me and still raving about the Ginger Toffees. This was just one point of value. How could you provide those 12 points of value for your clients?

Sales copywriting

If you're not a natural copywriter, it's worth working with someone trained professionally in producing sales-focused literature. I'm not talking about someone to check over your grammar & punctuation; I'm talking about someone who knows how to motivate customers. This is called sales copywriting. It's similar to when you see a sensationalist headline on the internet or newspaper; you'll click the headline or buy it to read it, and that decision is based solely on what that headline says. Very powerful.

The five motivators of behaviour tied to sales copywriting are fear, love, greed, guilt, and pride. If you tap into any of these, your sales copy will be more effective.

Pricing strategies

Various pricing strategies should be considered part of the overall client acquisition strategy. You can use multiple strategies based on how you wish to position the business. One strategy is to use a low price to secure the client, then aim to raise prices or increase the client's lifetime value by upselling other products later.

Another strategy used across some industries is to '*buy*' a client by bidding at cost or below cost price. This is usually done to build market share quickly and knock out competitors. This will only work if it's consistent over time and you have limited competition, assuming those competitors don't have more extensive resources to use the strategy and remove *YOU* from the market.

If done consistently and you can finance any loss, it could be a way to dominate your market while attracting staff from your competitors as they start to reduce in size due to contract loss.

Case study: Narcotics industry

You can learn a lesson about business in any industry - including the illegal ones.

Whilst I wasn't directly involved in the illegal narcotics industry, I grew up around people who were. I witnessed things the average outsider wouldn't usually see simply by being in their environment. One of these people, though I didn't know it when I first met him, actually turned out to be one of the higher-profile '*kingpins*' of the '90s and '00s in the drug trade within the UK. I discovered this later on when I wasn't friends with him anymore.

I'd met him some 13 years earlier, as he was a joiner on a site where I was an Apprentice, & we'd worked together with his company on several construction projects up until that point. On reflection, it was interesting because when people knew I was associated with him, I started to get stopped & searched frequently. I'd get pulled to the side by nightclub bouncers as they searched for drugs in my pockets & wallet. I was well-known in the area at the time. I knew most of the police & nightclub bouncers through my connection with martial arts, as many of them were also members of the local martial arts club. Up until that time, I'd never been searched before. It's strange how your association with someone automatically makes people think about you in a certain way, for good or for bad.

In the illegal drug industry, there are several levels of the organization. You'll have the manufacturer- the person responsible for creating the product. You have the Kingpins, those that organize everything, whether nationally coordinating things or working on a local level running things in that area. You'll have the *'runners'* or *'traffickers'*; these people move the product across the country and locally take it to the street. Then there's the *'salesperson'*, this is the person on the street corner or in the nightclub toilets, and the one most people associate with being the *'drug dealer'*.

Do you know how so many people become addicted to drugs?

With hard drugs, a dealer will give someone a small amount, just enough to get them addicted to it, at a very low cost, sometimes even free of charge, provided as a *'gift'* from a friend. They create a customer for life.

With the softer, less addictive drugs, it works the same way, except this time, they're getting the individual addicted to the buzz, the feeling or experience the drug creates. Again, a low-cost introduction creates a long-term customer. Often, this builds that *'friendship bond'* between customer & dealer, which leads to the harder addictive drugs later on.

With the salesperson & runners, you might wonder why they stay involved in it, especially when they've already been caught & gone to prison for it. Like my friends from school, it offers a better lifestyle; they get a glimpse of what it could be like, whether it's giving them a nice car, a lovely apartment, or the latest gadgets. For some, they might already be addicted to the drugs themselves and do it to feed their habit. An addiction to the lifestyle is what gets the salespeople & runners hooked in.

But all of these lessons can be utilized in the business world, whether it's free trials or understanding how to recruit & motivate your staff.

Level seven: Client

Level seven in the Ten C's Framework™ is Client. The objective of this level is to sell more to your existing clients. This is my favourite stage in the entire framework. I think it's probably the easiest way to grow any business.

At this stage of the process, the idea is not to try and win new clients. This stage is focused on people you already know, people who have bought from you in the past, current or past customers.

How do you squeeze more juice from each of these customers?

We're going to look at this question in three areas.

- Existing clients
- Existing product offerings
- New product offerings

Existing clients

How many customers have you dealt with in the last twenty years in your business? My guess is, there's a few that haven't purchased in a while.

The first step is to identify every customer you've ever worked for and what offers they purchased from you.

Next, we identify when contracts expire, both for current clients and those we no longer serve. If there's no official expiry date, consider it annually from the date you last worked with them. Keep a note of these dates for every contract and client, putting them into your sales system or a spreadsheet. Ideally, you'll want to set an alert to notify you before the date so you can prepare a new proposal or arrange a renewal meeting with the client. I'd aim to start that conversation around four months before the date in your spreadsheet.

For those contracts, you've previously bid for but not won, or perhaps the contracts that you've lost the renewal to another provider, make a list of every contract, the approximate value, the expiry or renewal date, & the company you lost out to. Also, try to discover who, within that competitor company, is responsible for managing the bid and, likewise, the contract. Consider recruiting those who are more successful in the bid process to strengthen your own team. Having this type of knowledge could be helpful.

If the original was a one-off capital project rather than a monthly subscription or retainer-style contract, consider whether there might be a recurring revenue element later on and note the likely date that could occur. An example of this could be a new factory being built; at some point in the future, the factory will need various support functions, whether general maintenance, IT support, staff recruitment and payroll, or even just training. Many companies will have opportunities, so getting in early could be beneficial.

Creating the opportunity

One of the areas I struggle to understand is why a company sits back and waits for a client to come to them. I'm a big believer in creating an opportunity for them to work with you.

An example of creating an opportunity could be if you have a client who has stated their intention to grow. Let's imagine that the client is a hotel operator. The ideal way to help them succeed would be to provide a 'ready to go' new hotel location. That can mean anything from identifying a new site to building a new property. Why wait for them to initiate with you? Why can't you be the person that helps them get everything they want?

Existing product offerings

The next step at this level is to identify your product offerings. Think about this in a very granular sense. For example, the offerings of an accountant wouldn't be generalized *'accountancy services'*. That would be a very high-level summary of what they provide. Their product offerings would be broken down into much greater detail than just the service category.

They might include
- Registered Address
- Outsourced CFO
- Payroll processing
- Credit control
- Self-employed tax filing
- Software set up

An easy way to do this is to consider what someone might search online for if they were looking for help with a particular problem. Likewise, the products wouldn't just be limited to *'overnight accommodation'* for a hotel. It would include all the *'pieces'* to that experience. It would consist of Swimming facilities, a Shower experience, a Gym, a Sauna, a Lounge area, and Valet parking. Then, it might go even deeper when considering the food &

beverage offering, breaking each menu item into individual products. If the business provides excursions or events, they're product offerings too. The idea is to list all those things they would be looking for.

Product staircase

The next thing you should do is consider what I call the Product Staircase. The Product Staircase is a system of creating products designed to build trust & credibility in your business.

There are three different levels of products, generally at various price points. The first level is usually free, or less than £10. The second level product is usually an educational product informing the client how to achieve what they want, doing it by themselves; this might be a training course. The third level product is the fully *'done for you'* solution. This is your core product. There are variations on this product staircase, & each type of business will differ slightly in what each product level provides. Some people use different prices as their levels, while others add a fourth product level, high-margin upsell products. High-margin upsell products are sold to customers after they've purchased your core product; an example would be a hotel selling an excursion or a massage treatment.

Product service levels

Another way to break down each product offering is by service levels. This is the typical bronze, silver, and gold model. Typically, the silver service level will be the one you expect the client to choose. The gold level covers all of the bells and whistles of the service, and hence, the price reflects that level of service. Likewise, the bronze level is the most basic level of service; this is the absolute bare minimum.

'Would you like a massage whilst I file your company accounts, sir?'

The good thing about this model is that you're giving them options; you can ramp up your profit margins with the gold level, as it's something that can't be easily compared with your competitors' pricing.

An advanced version of this might be to let your client cherry-pick exactly which options they want to include in their contract. This works best if you can do it instantly, give them the quote, and have them sign up there and then, much like when you buy car insurance online.

Product packaging

It's not just Mars bars and tins of Baked Beans that need to look good when they're packaged. All products, including service offerings, need to look attractive. They need product branding and offer what the client is specifically looking for. Each product offering should have its own dedicated webpage, too.

Low-profit products

After doing the work in the intelligence section, you'll know how much Gross Profit margin you make from every product offering. Whilst you may not be able to drop product offerings from your lineup, you may sell higher-margin products to your clients as part of a more extensive support package. This should take a low-profit client and make them more profitable. Which high-profit products could you offer to your customers?

New product offerings

Have you ever profiled each of your competitors to discover their offerings? Comparing your findings to those of your own business might highlight some gaps you might be missing out on. Suppose you're looking at your average local competitors. In that case, the chances are they'll look the same as you. Still, if you're looking at the exception, the one-off provider disrupting the market, or perhaps one of the national providers, you'll notice a big gap between what you provide and what they provide - or how they position their offerings.

Be honest with yourself. It's got to be a yes or no answer. Are they providing more than you, or are they providing something different to you? Don't fall into the trap of using excuses like *'Yes, they provide more than us, but they are bigger'*, *'Yes, but they're licensed for X services'*, or *'We don't have that type of experience'*.

There are two ways to look at this. First, if you've identified a gap, you probably have a few ideas of where to start when it comes to creating new product offerings for your clients. Second, if your local competitors are providing the exact same as you, imagine how much extra business you could attract when you start doing something they aren't.

What else are your clients buying?

By analyzing each of your clients, you might discover they're buying some product offerings related to your own. Don't rule anything out at this stage; make a note of it. You may hit on something that you could provide them with, that fits all these potential gaps well. Likewise, you might identify a new route to sell your product offerings to other new clients.

After you've examined each customer individually, it's time to consider those suggestions.

We'll consider these potential products that we can integrate into the business and have customers buy from us.

Cross-sell matrix

Now that we've identified all our product offerings and current and previous customers, we can put this information into the Cross-sell matrix.

The idea is to list all customers in the left-hand column and all product offerings, including service levels, across the top. Where a customer has a current contract for a product offering, you'll travel horizontally from the client name and vertically down from the Product until both paths cross. You'll shade it green in this matrix cell and enter the contract value. You could also include the contract expiry date.

When a contract has expired or been lost, you shade the cell orange with the approximate value & the expiry date, or just a date you'll follow up with the customer.

You leave the cell blank for all those customers who have yet to purchase a product. You can focus on selling these unsold product offerings to these cells. It would be a good idea to divert sales efforts away from trying to find new clients and instead focus on filling up these empty cells in the matrix. It costs you almost nothing to sell to these customers as you've already built their trust, so you should be able to substantially increase your bottom line profits with every sale.

This is an excellent activity for an account manager, as they've most likely built a relationship over time with each customer. Running a campaign for each product offering and targeting empty or orange cells helps remind clients that you're still alive and provides much more than they've already purchased.

Franchising & licensing

Let's talk briefly about franchising and licensing. There are two sides to franchising and licensing. Firstly, you franchise or license something within your own business and sell it to other firms like yours. The second is when you buy a franchise or license so you can sell someone else's Product to your client base.

If you choose to buy a franchise or license, remember how much time and effort went into creating that product offering and proving demand for it in the market. By investing in such an opportunity, you can sell it from day one without worrying about the risk of spending the next 18 months creating it yourself, which could cost a lot more than the franchise or license fee and have no guarantee of earning you a return on your investment. It already has proven demand with much less risk with an existing franchise or licence.

In every business, the best strategy is to have a portfolio of product offerings that you can sell to your existing customers. These include your original product offerings, franchised product offerings, licenced product offerings, and product joint ventures that you create and deliver alongside other partners.

Case study: Fire & security provider

In 2002, our contracting business was approached by one of the largest fire and security companies in the world. At the time, they operated from a handful of core offices across the country and were trying to expand their business reach into other locations with a local focus. Their strategy was to collaborate with certain companies across the UK, helping them roll out their brand on a local level.

They approached us. At the time, we covered the North Western quarter of Scotland, around 25% of the country's land mass, and our clients were the type of buildings they were looking for—Hotels, care homes, public buildings, new-build housing, etc.

While we provided some fire and security-related services, they weren't a big portion of our business. We planned to build that part of the business, establishing a dedicated fire and security division within the business, so the timing was perfect—actually freakishly perfect. I think the planets were aligned.

The arrangement was that we'd run two businesses: our existing business and a 50/50 Joint venture operating a separate Fire and security business under our partner's brand. We'd keep our own business branding but also use their branding. We'd use our staff to deliver every enquiry they received from new clients, and they'd train our staff in installing and maintaining their equipment.

It was a great opportunity. We were the only company that could service and install their systems for hundreds of miles. We'd also be responsible for managing their existing rural contracts, which they'd built up across the area. This created an opportunity for us to sell our existing services to their clients but also attracted new clients who otherwise wouldn't have come to us.

This was borrowed credibility from an international brand. As part of the arrangement, we had unlimited support to deal with any technical issues. We had access to people from their head office and manufacturing facility who could answer any query.

To be a part of the Joint Venture, there was a financial investment on our part, & we'd cash flow any operations that came through the JV company. It was a great model.

Level eight: Compensation

Level eight in the Ten C's Framework™ is called Compensation. The objective at this level is to improve profit margins at the delivery stage of the customer buying process.

For non-accountants, without getting too anal about it, the gross profit is what you have left after you've delivered the '*product*' to your customer. It includes the variable costs directly associated with delivery, which usually only occur when you have a customer. These variable costs generally increase directly to how many customers you have or how much they spend. It doesn't consider overhead or the business' operating expenses. An example for a hotel, one of the variable costs is the laundry costs; if a guest stays in the hotel, towels and sheets will need to be washed, but if there's no guests, there's no laundry cost.

How could you improve the profit margins on delivery? The simple answer is to increase charge-out prices or reduce delivery costs (or both). In this chapter, we'll look at a few strategies for doing that.

Increase prices

You might reject this option, especially if you're locked in a price battle with your competitors. Bear with me, though, because if that's the case, you need to consider what I'm about to say, more than the other strategies I'll discuss.

A customer will buy based on *the perception of value*. Most of the time, this comes down to how you package the product up.

Example.

When you buy Baked beans from the supermarket, let's assume you're buying at the premium end of the market. What's the primary factor that makes you choose one brand over another?

I'll tell you. It's 100% down to how it looks. Compare this to the cheaper *'own brand'* beans with the white label and plain text.

But what if I told you that those beans in the *'cheap tin'* are manufactured in the same factory as the more expensive tins? Tesco and Aldi don't have their own food manufacturing & packaging factory. Instead, they commit to an existing factory to buy a huge quantity, packaged under their brand (white labelling), at a considerable discount. You're buying the same product; it's just repackaged. And it can be the same in your own business.

Repackaging your products

Repackaging your *'products'* can mean anything from changing a colour scheme and logo font to giving something a dedicated product name or bundling multiple products together. By bundling products together, a customer can't easily compare your offering on price alone.

You can bundle in some products that the customer won't even use. They'll buy because they see enhanced value, but if they never use those extras, you're getting paid for them, but you don't have any cost of delivering them. This strategy is all about increasing the perception of value.

If you can increase your sales prices by 5%- 10%, it's unlikely that your customers will notice it too much, but that price increase will flow straight to your bottom line. If you're already operating on low margins, that could mean doubling your profit figure without doing anything else.

Now let's look at the opposite route - How to reduce delivery costs.

Here's a few ideas about how you might reduce delivery costs

- Is the delivery process efficient, or are there bottlenecks?
- Are people standing waiting for others to finish before performing their own tasks?
- Negotiating more significant discounts with suppliers
- Do your staff have any ideas on how to reduce costs?
- Measure & reduce unproductive time
- How do you control purchasing?
- Can you reduce wastage?
- Can some tasks be automated?

Systemize the business

I first learned about this strategy when I was 21, installing cabling into new-build houses as an electrician.

There were two identical houses, but one was completed in about 4 hours, whereas mine took almost two days. It all came down to working to a system—doing everything in a particular order and in a specific way. When I was taught the system, my next house was completed in 4 hours. I then taught other people the system, and they, too, delivered in 4 hours. There are considerable time savings just from being organized a certain way.

This all adds to the business's Gross profit, and every business has processes happening every single day. If you haven't found the most efficient way to deliver each task, this is your starting point for this strategy.

Client / Contract analysis

Analyze each client or contract in your business. You'll typically find some that contribute very little gross profit to the company. A few might even be negative, meaning they drain the company's profit. You really have two options. You can repackage to increase your prices and, subsequently, your profit margins, or, more likely, if it doesn't affect the rest of the business, you can just stop accepting them as customers.

Example.
An example is a business my family set up - a guest house providing overnight accommodation. With this business, they found a specific type of customer would cost them considerably more to deliver than all the rest. This type of customer would stay only for a single night, which meant bed linen & towels had to be washed daily. But in addition, they also seemed to make a lot more mess. The bedroom would be *'trashed'*, the breakfast area would be left in a mess, and they'd

also seem to eat much more food than most other guests. All in all, it took a lot more work, & cost more to deliver to that type of customer.

Improve productivity

Sometimes, improving productivity means more than systemizing the business. Sometimes, it's just the wrong person in the wrong seat. Various profiling systems are available, but I recommend using the Wealth Dynamics profiling tool, as it's more actionable than others.

After you've got the right people in the right seats and systems in place, it might be even more beneficial to use technology to further improve productivity.
Imagine how much time was saved when car manufacturers started using robots to assist in the production line. It's the same in your own business. It doesn't have to mean using robots, but even something as small as using an app to reduce time

spent performing a particular process, for example. Anywhere that duplication is found, such as form filling, presents a potential improvement for productivity & efficiency.

Case study: Lifecycle pricing

Working with a forward-thinking regional hotel group, they had always looked for innovative ways to improve the customer experience. Before we started working with them, they'd done very little maintenance or refurbishment of their buildings. This meant that after 30+ years of use, things were pretty tired, & they faced high capital replacement costs. Their plan was to build the group further by acquiring a number of other hotels; it came down to a choice for them - acquisitions or refurbishment.

By viewing them as a long-term growing partner, we decided to approach their project requirements differently.

Firstly, there was one hotel that needed complete electrical rewiring. Doing this in one go wasn't practical, as it would have cost them more than

£400k and closed the building for 4-6 months. For this project, we instead worked on a room-by-room basis; renovating each room meant the hotel could remain open, whilst the public areas could be worked on during the evenings & in the off-season. We estimated that each room would recoup the renovation cost within eight weeks, & so every time we completed a room, we gave the client three invoices, spreading the cost over the following three months. To finance this, the client was happy for us to increase our prices. This meant that our margins increased by around 25% after financing costs.

Level nine: Capital

Level nine in the Ten C's Framework™ is Capital. The objective of this level is to improve the overall profit figure in the business after considering operating expenses and overhead.

EBIT (Earnings Before Interest & Tax) is the general measure used to measure a business's profitability when it receives investment or is sold. In this chapter, we'll look at a few strategies to increase this number.

M&A (Mergers & Acquisitions)

M&A is a strategy that can be used at various stages in the framework. For example, if you want to add a new sector to the Level one Audience, then acquiring a business that already serves that new target sector is a good strategy to follow. But M&A is also a strategy to increase the EBIT figure and is a major strategy used by publicly traded companies. Adding other businesses to yours, either through buying or merging with them, helps you increase the value multiple. Suppose you find a business that complements yours. In that case, cross-selling between both companies also brings additional benefits and potentially reduces some overhead costs.

Trim the fat

When was the last time you did an expense reduction audit? I learnt this strategy from dealing with distressed businesses. Most businesses incur expenses over time which they forget about. Six years later, they're still paying for them. It could be software licenses, magazine subscriptions, memberships, or something bigger.

If your staff have their own expense accounts, they probably aren't spending money as if it were their own. As a business grows, it brings in new people. Those people bring their bad habits that infect the rest of the company.

Finally, regarding this strategy, I've found that people are generally lazy when it comes to spending other people's money. If your staff comes from the corporate or public sector, their habits are probably even worse.

Lean staffing

How lean is your operating team? Does every manager need a Personal Assistant, or could one PA service everyone? I hope you get my point.

Could a piece of software replace a member of staff? I once met the owner of a distressed business who said that rather than utilizing software, he'd just employ a new member of staff. The software costs were £6,000 a year, whereas it cost him about £20,000 to hire the staff member.

As I've come into contact with so many businesses over the years, I've noticed a trait shared across many of them. I've noticed that, as a company grows, it seems to employ people who aren't as productive as they could be. I always remember one business I worked alongside; they employed a project manager. Still, that manager would take half his day to write a 2 paragraph email. He was a nice guy, & he knew how to manage people. Still, his productivity issue stemmed from his earlier life experiences. His main problem was trying to be perfect to protect himself. Crossing every 'T' and dotting every 'I'. He came from the corporate world, where he'd been so used to '*covering his back*', & so this perfection was his defence tactic. But the defence cost the business much wasted time, as he formulated, then reviewed, then re-formulated his email to ensure nobody could '*get him*'.

Hiring consultants

This is a strategy I've learnt from working with private equity. It comes down to how expenses in the business are recorded in the financial accounts. Rather than employing staff directly to perform specific tasks, if the task is something that's, let's say, a '*one-off*' event, by hiring an external consultant to deliver it, the cost of that consultant is considered to be non-recurring and so it doesn't reduce the EBIT figure like an employee would do.

Shared resource

Just after the 2009 recession, I was involved in setting up a *'shared service business'*. It's more common in the charity or public sector. Still, the basic concept is that several organizations transfer all their back office staff into a centralized office. A new business entity is established, & those staff are *'sold'* by the hour to whoever needs them. In this case, it was supplied only to internal organizations. Still, in some instances, the shared services business could also sell externally to new clients.

By operating this model, each organization pays for only what it needs, & when it needs extra short-term support, it can tap into those other staff from the other organizations.

Now, to copy this model in the private sector, you need a number of businesses willing to participate. In all likelihood, the time involved in setting it up would prevent it from happening.

However, you can still use a similar model to reduce your overhead costs, turning that cost centre into a revenue centre. I'm sure some of your supply chain might need HR or Finance department support. By providing that support to them, you can create a profit on a resource that would otherwise just be a drain on the business.

Shared premises

Something I've learnt through the mergers and acquisitions process is that the larger a business gets, the more negotiation or buying power it has. The same rule applies to business premises. Take a typical office space as one example.

A small office space, say 1,000 sq ft, might cost £25 / sq ft to rent. But if you scale that space requirement to 10,000 sq ft, you might reduce rental costs to £20 / sq ft. I've seen much larger buildings go for as low as £13 / sq ft.

So there are two options for this.

Option 1: Find other businesses to share with

Option 2: Buy a larger building and sublet it to other businesses, potentially paying for your share of the rent.

This is effectively what companies like Regus do. It doesn't matter what type of premises you need. If you're a hotel, you can share hotel space with another '*hospitality*' business, i.e., a restaurant operator, gym operator, etc. Likewise, a manufacturing company shares space with other manufacturing processes.

Perhaps you could rent some of your space to your supply chain, too. In our contracting business, we rented office and workshop space from one of our hotel group clients. They previously had no use for this building, and it was just lying empty, so we took it over, fitted it out, and then rented it from them.

Cost drivers in a business

Some of the typical cost drivers in a business are:
- Economies of scale
- Capacity utilization - Are all your staff & resources fully utilized
- Learning curves - Has someone already walked your path, so you don't need to make the same mistakes - this is relevant to new product offerings
- Location - Local costs, salaries, transport costs, cost of living, etc
- Purchasing - How good are you at negotiating
- Operating efficiency
- Investment into automation
- Investment into training
- Waste management
- Premise costs

Level ten: Compound

Level ten in the Ten C's Framework™ is called Compound. The objective at this level is to increase the value of your assets.

How much are your assets worth? You might typically think about how much your house is worth or your shares in *Google* if you have them. Still, chances are, you don't think about what your business is worth or the strategies you might use to drive that value increase.

I use the word loosely, but this chapter is about using various strategies to *'manipulate'* the system to increase the value of your business.

When I talk about manipulating the system, this isn't about doing something dodgy that might cause the tax inspector to come calling. This is just about knowing the rules of the game, & then playing to those rules as best you can to win that game. There's nothing new in what I'm about to share; it's just that most of the business community has never been shown this stuff, but those who are *'professionals'* in the business community and those employed to maximize investment returns use these strategies daily. Other people have been using these strategies in various formats for decades.

The average small business might slave away for a year and only earn £200,000 in profit. The strategies I share in this chapter will show how some people make more than this in a single deal.

I hope you understand how the market values your business and how a slight adjustment can shift its worth dramatically.

Grouping

So, a traditional form of grouping is called a '*roll-up*'. Roll-ups have been around the world of private equity for over a century. The main process is to start with one company. This is usually a larger '*platform*' company, to which the platform company will then go out & acquire many other companies within its industry. This is done to consolidate a fragmented industry before selling the combined group. The platform company will usually acquire each target company before '*rolling*' them into their group structure.

A roll-up is just one form of grouping.

Another model of grouping, created by one of my business partners, is called '*Agglomeration*'. With this model, you group several private businesses under a group holding vehicle. No money exchanges hands, and each company continues to operate independently of the rest. Each business owner has the option to unwind from the structure in the future.

The main reason and benefit of using this model is the size of the combined group. The combined scale means each company within the group can bid for much larger contracts and benefit from other synergies that would typically only be achieved through a more formal merger or acquisition process. A side benefit to this structure is that it also creates a vehicle for selling a business at a much greater valuation multiple than if each company were sold as a single company.

Consider a small local business as an example. With approximately 98.7% of SME businesses listed for sale never actually achieving a sale, it can be challenging, almost impossible, to sell a small business. There isn't a large pool of buyers queuing to buy small businesses. Let's use hotels as an example because they're very visual. Still, it's the same scenario for most types of small businesses.

A small hotel probably won't have a full management team, especially at the finance director, Operations director, and CEO levels. It might not even have a full-time hotel manager. This makes it unattractive to a professional buyer (the type with an abundance of cash and motivation to invest it), as they'd essentially be buying themselves a full-time job. This means it's left to those buyers with little or no money.

Now, this type of business has an asset. It has a product or experience, a database of clients, a supply chain, and might also have a physical asset in terms of the actual Property from which the business operates. Thousands of companies are like this in every sector, all in the same boat. To achieve a sale, they must rethink and repackage how the opportunity is structured.

Now imagine if we took one hotel in every town, say 30 in total. Each hotel would be *'packaged'* to be part of a *'collection'*. It could be the *'City Collection'*, or it might be a collection of country houses with golf courses packaged up as *'The Country Collection'*.

As a one-off hotel, they aren't attractive to a professional buyer. However, as a group of 30 independent hotels with £25 million in revenue, larger hotel groups or private equity buyers will become very interested. This is essentially a roll-up, but without any upfront money changing hands.

Rather than a private equity fund doing it and making 100% of the profit in the process, with this model, the extra uplift in value is shared between each hotel owner.

Each business operates independently, as its own limited liability company, and continues to operate under its branding. The objective here is to package several companies into a *'wrapper'*, with the sole intention not to operate them as a group but to sell them to a professional buyer at an increased valuation based on that combined scale.

The only caveat to doing this is that each business within the structure needs to do some prep work. From dealing with hundreds of companies over the years, I've found that 95% have very poor systems & conformity regarding being *'investment ready'* or just having themselves *'sorted'*. For some, it could mean just keeping their monthly management accounts up to date. Still, for others, it can go much deeper, such as setting up computer systems and having proper legal agreements with staff & suppliers. For this reason, it's usually easier to have an external third party put it all together and take care of finding a buyer & managing that process.

The mainstream *'business for sale'* brokers don't get involved in this type of project; it's too time-consuming for them and most don't have the skillset or experience to put it together correctly.

The final step is to put a senior management team across the group. These are temporary, as they'll most likely be replaced when the sale is completed, especially if the buyer already has investments in that sector. This management team will include a CEO, COO, & CFO for the group. They aren't there to bark orders at you; their role is to put it all together, make sure everything goes smoothly with the sale, and, most importantly, put all the paperwork together, ready for the due diligence process.

Whilst we've used the example of grouping hotels, the same process can be followed with most small businesses, whether children's nurseries or plumbing contractors, so long as you have a professional buyer investing in that sector and a team to put it all together.

Management team

Did you know a business reliant on its owners is worth less than a business with a management team? Regardless of whether you wish to sell in the future, this strategy also provides you with some protection.

Imagine if tomorrow you leave the house, have a car crash, and can't work for six months. If your business relies on you for ANYTHING, there's a strong chance it won't be trading when you've fully recovered. I know a business owner this happened to, so please don't think it'll never happen. Murphy's law says it probably will.

It's crucial to replace yourself in the business. Make the company less reliant on you.

The next thing to consider is succession.

Over 70% of businesses in the Western economies are owned & operated by people who will reach retirement age by 2025. Who's in line to take your place? Do they have the expertise & drive to continue in your footsteps? What can you do to prepare them now?

Share arbitrage

We've already discussed the value multiple. Do you know the fastest way to grow shareholder value for a public listed company, is to buy private companies?

Let's say you're a public company, and your shares are trading at a 10x multiple. That means your shares are worth ten times its profit.

If you buy a private company at a 4x multiple (4 times profit), say £1m profit. That means you pay £4m to acquire it. But after you've added that £1m profit into your own business, that £1m is now worth ten times the profit. You've increased the value of the public business by £10m, but it only cost you £4m. This is called share arbitrage, and it's why public companies use M&A (Mergers & Acquisitions) as one of their core growth strategies.

However, you don't need to be a public company to use this strategy. The same approach can be applied to a smaller private company. Buying a business at a 3x multiple could push the combined business value to a 4-5x multiple.

M&A

We've touched on it several times, but I want to go deeper now. Many people will say that M&A is the only strategy for growing a small business. This is a slightly naive mindset.

An M&A strategy should be viewed as something other than an easy, quick-fix answer to growing your business; *'doing a deal in an afternoon'* is rarely the case. Closing a suitable deal will take 6-9 months of full-time work. When we start cold in the acquisition process, we typically begin with around 400 target companies to close a deal with one. What we'll experience when we begin this process, from that original 400 companies, is that we might have interest from about 40 of those. Rates vary between 4% - 10%. After initial discussions, you very quickly disqualify 80% of those interested parties. It'll either be a lack of motivation on their part, failing to send more information, or you'll discover they aren't a good fit for your own business. This leaves around four companies from that original pool, which we'll typically meet face to face, & then present our offer based on the numbers they've provided.

I often hear stories about people buying a business. Still, on analysis, that deal adds no value to their existing business. They've done a deal, so they can say they've done it. It makes no strategic sense to me. It's a waste of your time, money & energy. So, what is the perfect deal?

When most people think about buying or merging with another company, their default is to think about their competitors. In truth, this adds very little potential to your business. The ideal scenario should be to consider adding a new sector, product, or geography to your business. So, let's consider an example.

Example.

A plumbing company based in Manchester, UK. Currently serves clients in the Hospitality sector within a 50-mile radius. The ideal acquisition would be a company providing a complementary product, perhaps an electrical contractor serving clients in the Manufacturing sector, & based in Leeds, UK. This means it could sell electrical services to its hospitality clients, & vice versa. It also means both companies could access a new geographic coverage area, covering the North West & Yorkshire. Within 2-3 years of completing this acquisition, you could expect both businesses to have rinsed out those synergies & achieved around 4x growth, solely through internal cross-selling.

Joint venture partnerships

The final strategy I want to consider in this chapter is Joint venture partnerships. Collaborating with other businesses could achieve everything we've discussed in this book. Some people in the business community are much better at doing what they do than you will ever be. You're an expert at what you do. I'm an expert at what I do. If I tried to do something I'd not done before, I'd probably get terrible results, which would waste my time and money.

Take one example. At a certain time in my life, I considered myself very good at winning public sector contracts. I was winning an average of 89% of the contracts I tendered at that time. So I decided to work with a few companies, whereby I'd bid on their behalf, & they'd deliver their service. Rather than paying me by the hour or per tender, I agreed to take a share of revenue from every tender I won. This meant the arrangement worked well for both parties. If I were successful, my share was far more than what I might have earned the traditional way, & for them, they had access to contracts they otherwise wouldn't have had, without paying someone by the hour going through a trial and error process.

After working on many similar arrangements, some going well, & some not so well, I learnt a few lessons about the best way to set these arrangements up. The first thing to do is to identify what each party brings to the arrangement. In the above case, the experience/skillset, & delivery capability were the two main pieces. Then, it has to be laid out what responsibility each party will have, & how each will be rewarded. Everything should be formalized, written down, agreements signed, companies set up, etc. People tend to have very short memories as soon as they have the money in their hands. The project needs someone driving it on both sides; otherwise, it tends to run dry when one side gets busier.

Finally, there has to be some buy-in. A joint venture shouldn't be treated differently than any other type of investment, whether buying a business, a franchise, a licence, or anything else. On a few occasions, I've invested a lot of my time & money into a JV project, only for the other party to have zero buy-in, & therefore not follow through on their responsibilities to see things through. It doesn't matter what that buy-in is, but it has to be significant enough for both sides to feel the need to follow through.

Case study: University business services

In 2016, we worked with a University to determine whether we could find an alternative model to generate revenue streams for them. A change in legislation for international students had reduced their traditional revenue streams, which made up a large proportion of their income.

At the time, the University employed around 2,500 staff members, of which at least half were involved in non-lecturing support roles in HR and recruitment, marketing, facilities management, finance, etc.

After considering various opportunities, we examined several strategies in depth. The first was a product strategy, which involved packaging the various business support services to sell them to external clients.

The concept of the opportunity was to sell business support services, such as marketing, IT support, HR, and facilities management, to other local businesses in the area. We'd create a tender pipeline, and with several large contracts already lined up, we projected it would bring an additional £240 million in revenue over ten years.

A side benefit of the project was that we'd employ university graduates within the new business, giving them valuable career experience while also developing relationships with local businesses we were serving and inviting them to join us on the University campus.

Our ten-year plan for the business was to relocate most of those non-core staff based within the campus buildings into centralized purpose-built premises on the outskirts of the city. This would make it much easier for many to commute and lower the cost of premises. This would free up space that could be repurposed to generate additional revenue for the University while also reducing operating costs.

The bottleneck

Every business has at least one Bottleneck that prevents it from achieving growth. In this chapter, we'll look at a few of the more common bottlenecks to be aware of as you start your growth journey.

Property

A massive bottleneck for many '*physical*' businesses is Property. Whether you're a shipping and distribution company, a construction company, or a hotel operator, Property (or space) will eventually prevent the business from growing further. Let's look at two examples of this.

Example 1 - Your office.
If an office space can house 15 staff at its maximum capacity, this is an infrastructure bottleneck. What happens when you need that 16th member of staff?

Does that mean you need a whole new office to meet that expected future demand, or is there another strategy you could use, at least in the short term?

Example 2 - A hotel.

A hotel is limited by how much it can sell. If a hotel has 50 bedrooms, it can only ever sell 50 bedrooms. If it sells more than 50 bedrooms, can it set up temporary beds in the dining room? Of course not. This is a delivery bottleneck.

What strategies could you use to increase that capacity, and when is the best time to start that process?

Machinery / Plant / Vehicles

Many businesses use machinery, plants, or vehicles. A manufacturing business, for example, might use specialist equipment or tooling that can operate at a specific capacity. It might create 1,000 widgets a day at total capacity. That's great if you're only operating at 600 widgets currently, but what happens when demand reaches 1200 widgets a day? The business might lose its reputation for not delivering orders on time.

In a commercial kitchen, the chef's ability to cook as many chickens as possible is limited to the workspace, the number of kitchen staff, and how large the rotisserie is. Likewise, suppose your business relies on vehicles, such as a construction or haulage business. In that case, it can only grow as large as those trucks allow it to.

What's your strategy for getting around these bottlenecks?

Supply chain

Finding good, reliable suppliers can take more work than many realize. When you find one, you want to keep them, but this creates a supply chain bottleneck.

Around 80% of small businesses don't wish to grow. As your business grows, if your supply chain has this '*anti-growth*' mindset, you've got to find a way around it.

Some businesses invest in or acquire a supplier to control this potential Bottleneck.

Staffing

We can look at the staffing bottleneck from two viewpoints.

The first is the staff you employ. Each of these people has a maximum capacity or output, regardless of what job they perform. We only have 24 hours in a day, and some roles might be missing in your business completely.

Does each staff member have the skills, expertise, training, knowledge, and, most importantly, the ability to take the business to its desired future?

I've learned that most people get comfortable at a certain level, and that level is right for them. I have a friend who's very good at growing start-up technology companies. He's grown a few into major players. Still, he hates the bureaucracy of working in a corporate environment, and so he resigns from each business when it reaches that level. It's the same with your staff.

Your current staff can cope if you desire to grow by 10%. But if you plan to expand your business to 10 times its current size, then most of the staff you employ now, probably won't be around when you get there.

The second viewpoint we need to consider is the owner.

If you're the owner and currently work in the business, you're the bottleneck. Believe it or not, there are people in the market who are better than you at 80% of what you do daily.

It's like the introverted bookworm emerging from their dark cupboard to become the best used-car salesperson on the planet. No matter how hard they work or how much training they receive, they'll never be that person.

Losing a job title doesn't mean losing control. You're the shareholder, and everyone else works *FOR YOU*. You'll always be at the top, regardless of your job title. Move aside and let someone else improve your business performance while you focus on what you're good at.

The problem is, you're probably reading this, chuckling away to yourself in agreement, thinking, *'Yes, that's not me, but I know what you're talking about; this doesn't apply to me, ha ha ha'.* It takes having an external person, someone who doesn't care about hurting your feelings, stroking your ego, or climbing your career ladder, to tell you the truth and what's actually in YOUR best interests and those of the company.

Capital

One final bottleneck to consider is capital. It's what keeps the wheels spinning. The biggest reason for a company failing is running out of cash. Whilst you might plan to grow the business, you'll probably need capital to achieve your ambitions. Whether from internal reserves or external sources such as equity investment. It could be for cash flow, renting larger premises, buying more equipment, buying stock, or recruiting new staff.

Fixing the bottleneck

Regardless of what bottlenecks exist in your business, I've found that the best way to move forward is to perform a *GAP analysis*. This means creating a picture of what the company will look like at a future point and then doing the same for what it looks like now. By comparing the two pictures, you can identify the '*GAP*' and plan how to fill each gap.

If we consider staffing, for example, we start with an organizational chart that shows all the staff needed to operate the business at a future date. Then, we do the same again, plotting all the staff and their current roles. There will inevitably be a difference.

Suppose you feed this into other business areas, such as office space demand. In that case, it'll inform you about other 'gaps' or potential bottlenecks that need fixing. But it all starts with where you expect growth—in most cases, customer sales—and feeds across all business areas.

The secret ingredients

After working with many businesses, I've discovered that I could provide each of them with the contents of this book. Still, only a few of them would achieve anything with it. It made me question why some get results, yet others don't. After many years of contemplating this, I stumbled across that elusive answer. It had eluded me because it had always been something that came naturally to me; I did it automatically, & therefore, I just expected that other people would do that, too.

I call it the '*secret ingredients*' because it's a secret to most people.

To make your plans successful, you'll need eight core ingredients, three of which we've already covered.

- A system or Framework (the roadmap)
- People
- Funding
- Share the spoils
- Focus
- Mindset
- Collective mind
- Momentum

Let's look at the other five to understand them deeper.

Share the spoils

Suppose you understand that everything in a metaphysical sense is a vibration, & that everything you encounter is made up of tiny atoms, each vibrating to a particular frequency. In that case, you'll also understand that money & people are also reacting to a certain vibration.

The problem with many people is that they're greedy. Whilst they say they aren't, I've witnessed it over & over again: as soon as money enters their grasp, the green mist descends, & they want it all. It often reminds me of Golem with his *'my precious'* in the Lord of the Rings movie trilogy. The problem with this attitude is that many players were involved in helping you get what you wanted. If you cut them out of the spoils, they won't help you again; they'll more likely work against you. If you share the spoils, it incentivizes every player to dig even deeper next time.

We can see examples of the most successful empires built throughout history. Those who survived for centuries did so because they shared their spoils of war. Take the Romans, for example. When each soldier retired from fighting, they received a piece of land from the empire. It's the same with the British Empire, which gave each of its generals land after each conquest.

When discussing sharing the spoils, I don't mean giving them 1% while you keep 99%. Do you know the real meaning behind Charles Dickens's novel *Scrooge*? It's not about Christmas. The real meaning is about greed and how greed destroys people's lives, including those holding the spoils.

Focus

Every action you perform represents intention and the energy you transmit into a future picture you're creating. That vision you created for your life is like a picture you've painted in your mind. The *ONLY* way you'll create this is through focused action. If your mind's scattered, you're jumping from task to task; your energy is also scattered. It's like your energy is being frittered away; there's no momentum being created because you aren't focusing on that vision for your life & business.

So, where should you focus? Well, you should always keep that end vision in your mind. Everything you do should move you closer to that vision. If *EVERY* action isn't moving you toward that vision, it's moving you away. Hence, you're scattering energy that you've previously built up. It all comes down to intention. Doing everything on purpose, like you designed it that way. One way to think about focus is to step into your future self, the self that's already achieved what you wanted, and from that place, think about the major actions you took to get there. From this place, you can also consider the activities you're doing now, & ask your future self, are these the right activities? Are they getting you there in the most efficient way? If you used the 10x rule, where you increase your future vision by ten times, would your activities be the same as you'd use to achieve the 10x vision, or are you doing activities that don't matter?

Mindset

The biggest problem with people I've found is that they don't think big enough. This is what traps you into a life where you spend most of your energy settling for a hamster wheel. The education system discourages big thinkers, but the fact is, if we're all just balls of energy vibrating, then we can achieve anything that our minds can think of. I've lived out my childhood dreams and done things that other people told me I'd never do. Still, it all originated from having that thought of it being possible.

Forget about Negative Nelly or Distraction Dave; we don't care what they say; we don't care what they think of us and our plans. Why bother even telling them? Do you know how many people I tell about my 10-year life plan? Nobody. At best I share small pieces of it with one or two people. Those people will help me achieve a specific area of that plan. Suppose you start telling everyone about your vision. The typical reaction will be negative - *'Who does he think he is, to think he can do that!'* - I've been surrounded by these people my entire working life.

About 25 years ago, I worked with a guy every day who was employed as a labourer in our contracting business. He would always talk about how he'd like to do a property development one day. This wasn't such a giant leap of the imagination for me, as even though I was only 20 at the time, my family had been developing Property for generations, & we'd already built three big houses to that point since I'd left school. One day, I proposed a small project to him with the idea that we could work on it together. It was converting an old village dentist surgery into a two-bedroom bungalow. He immediately dismissed the idea, & said, *'Who do you think you are, Richard Branson?'*.

As soon as you stop caring what these muppets think of you, the more unrestricted you'll be, but until that time, don't tell them anything. When people show me how small they think, I struggle to be around them; it's like being in a hostile atmosphere.

The growth mindset

I sometimes suggest to business owners the idea of making themselves redundant. This scares some people; they see it from the eyes of a traditional employee. If you make yourself redundant in that sense, you no longer have a job, & you won't be able to pay your mortgage anymore. That's not what I'm talking about. Let me give you an example.

If you provide a service to a customer, you charge the customer £40 an hour for your time. You then pay yourself what's left of that £40 after you've paid business expenses. Let's say that is £15. If you employ someone else to provide that same service, let's assume the cost of employing that person is £10. By making yourself redundant, you're being paid £5 but doing nothing for it. With your free time, you can now go out & find another customer, & earn £5 from them too. This is the growth mindset. That would never have happened without replacing yourself, as you'd always be in that hamster wheel, too busy to think about other things.

The other option to replace yourself is to consider outsourcing it to someone else, a self-employed person, a freelancer, or even another company you choose to partner with. How you decide to do this will depend on the task the individual delivers.

The good thing about the outsourced route is that if it's task-based, you can work with them on a fixed fee basis rather than an open hourly or daily rate where the numbers can spiral out of control. This means they don't get paid until they deliver the result according to your quality & timeline criteria.

The collective mind

Believe it or not, there's a powerful hidden force called the collective mind that you can tap into to achieve anything you want in your business or personal life. If you imagine that it's just you thinking about your business vision, unless you're a magician, the energy you put out to the world through your focus, intention, and actions will be minimal.

But consider if 1000 people all think about the same thought, they all share the same picture. That picture will become a reality very quickly. This comes down to energy & intention being transmitted. Adding emotion to this thought enhances the energy level even further. To make this happen in your business, you need at least three people, all sharing the same vision, &

thinking about achieving that vision, each taking action toward that vision every day. The more people that follow this same routine, the more influential the collective mind is.

An excellent example of the collective mind is when the famous illusionist Derren Brown used the collective mind principle a few years ago to predict the lottery draw numbers. If you search online, you'll probably find a video recording. He collected a group of people and trained them on what to do over a short period. Over a week, they went through the process together, testing the theory, and then perfecting it. Ultimately, the group achieved five out of the six drawn lottery numbers, which was done live as the numbers were drawn. He concluded that, had the group been larger and with a little more time, they could have got all six numbers.

When multiple people perform specific actions or carry the same intention, this is called a ritual. On a metaphysical level, the energy created behind it is the equivalent of 2+2=96. If you can set this up so that all participants perform the act simultaneously, the outcome is even more intense.

What could you achieve if you *'set your mind to it?'*

Momentum

Finally, the last secret ingredient is simple, yet most never realize it. This is why the framework you've been learning about is called *'Momentum'*.
Imagine trying to move a large rock through a muddy field. At first, the rock will be tough to move, but as you maintain your routine, gradually, it moves much easier; it starts to move under its weight. Now, if you divert your focus somewhere else or stop moving it altogether, the rock will stop moving, and it'll be hard to get going again. This happens in a business; it needs an intense amount

of energy & intention to get it growing, but slowly, the amount of effort & energy required to keep it rolling reduces because it's moving under its own steam. Suppose you dedicate twelve months to growing your business, and you can get others along for the ride who share your vision. In that case, this will create so much Momentum that your business will experience a massive change. Progress might be slow initially, but perseverance is critical as Momentum is building behind the curtain. It might mean working a few late nights and weekends, but that dedication will be worth it.

Summary

So we're at the end of Part Two, The Ten C's Framework™. We've covered a lot, and with the strategies you've learnt, you can double the size of your business in the next 12-18 months.

As a guide to growing your business, you should intend to add every year:
- Add at least one new product offering
- Penetrate one new sector niche
- Add at least one new lead-generation method
- Acquire a complementary / competing company

To recap, the first area we examined during the Compass level was creating a roadmap that would take you where you want to go, using your business as the vehicle.

In the Community level, we looked at increasing the pond of potential clients we're working with and the best strategies. Then, we moved onto the Club level, considering the various strategies to get on the radar of those target clients, and create interest in working with us.

From the Club level, we looked at how to create credibility both Internally & externally in the eyes of the client. From the Credibility level, we looked at the Confidence level, how to close the sale and the various strategies to increase the sales conversion rate.

In level seven of the framework, we examined the easiest and fastest way to grow your business by adding new product offerings and selling more to your existing clients. In level eight, Compensation, we examined strategies to increase delivery-focused profit margins. Then, in the Capital level, we followed this up by using techniques to increase the business's EBIT level.

In level ten, the Compound level, we looked at strategies to multiply the value of our assets. In the final two chapters, we completed this learning journey by considering the potential bottlenecks you might face when you grow your business, & most importantly of all, we rounded it all off by talking through the eight secret ingredients that every business needs if they want to grow their business successfully.

Conclusion

Do you know when you read a celebrity's autobiography and learn they had a certain trigger event in their life that put them on the path to where they are now? Whether it was a chance meeting with someone or perhaps they were presented with an opportunity, looking back, they could pinpoint those events as pivotal and defining moments in their lives.

We all get those types of opportunities in life, but we don't see them as such at the time because they don't come with a pink bow and flashing lights attached, whether it's being offered a new job or another business opportunity.

This defining moment tells the universe whether you want it and whether you're willing to step up and take it. Things generally stay the same until we shift how we think and act. These opportunities put you on a different trajectory, and this is where the magic happens.

Most people don't take an opportunity when it's offered. This makes the difference between those who live their dream lives and those who don't. On your current trajectory, you might make a bit of money and live a comfortable life, but when you reach your final day and look back, will you be able to say you lived your dream life, or will you wake up ten years from now wondering *what if*?

These '*trigger*' moments might come from a random letter you receive through the mail, sparking your interest, but you fail to take it any further. You might need to make that phone call, but keep putting it off. This book wasn't written for everyone. It was written for just ONE person. If anything you've read in this book resonated with you, maybe that person is YOU.

To get started on your growth journey, this is YOUR pivotal moment. You have the tools and guidance you need all within this book. But you'll need to take focused action to receive the full value I encourage you to commit, setting aside time every week to focus on this. Start with every Friday afternoon, and aim to increase that time to the full day. Focus on completing one area at a time. This is the only way you'll reach your desired result.

For anyone serious about growing their business, I've created an online program which includes 29 hours of video content, along with templates you can use for each section of the Momentum Framework™. You can get access to the program by visiting the *Business Academy* section of my website.

If you want to access unique content or hear about the latest opportunities, projects or businesses I'm involved with, I'd encourage you to join my VIP club. It's free, and you can join it by signing up at my website, www.wayne-fox.co.uk

If you've got this far, I appreciate you spending this time with me. This book represents the conclusion of a 25-year chapter in my life, documenting the process for others to use long after I've left this world. As with you, the experiences I've gathered during this chapter of my story will guide us in what comes next.

About the author

Wayne Fox is a business re-ignitor, industry disruptor, commercial property developer, futurist, best-selling Author, & investor. Director of the Enyaw group, a UK-based investment firm that invests in *'freedom lifestyle'* ventures. He is experienced in achieving 7 & 8-figure revenue growth across previous SME ventures.

My online links:

Wayne Fox Website: www.wayne-fox.co.uk

Enyaw Group: www.enyawgroup.com

Enyaw Capital: www.enyawcapital.com

Enyaw Property: www.enyawproperty.co.uk

Linkedin: https://www.linkedin.com/in/waynefoxuk

Twitter: https://twitter.com/WayneFoxUK1

Instagram: https://www.instagram.com/waynefoxuk

Youtube: https://www.youtube.com/@WayneFoxUK

Udemy: https://www.udemy.com/user/wayne-fox-6

www.ingramcontent.com/pod-product-compliance
Lightning Source LLC
Chambersburg PA
CBHW050153230526
45470CB00001B/78